How to Be a Bad Christian

Finding God when you don't measure up

How to be a BAD Christian

Finding God when you don't measure up

Christopher Easley

How to Be a Bad Christian: Finding God When You Don't Measure Up

Copyright © 2019 by Christopher Easley

All rights reserved. No part of this book may be reproduced in any form without prior permission of the publisher.

Scripture quotations marked ESV are from the ESV® Bible (The Holy Bible, English Standard Version®), copyright © 2001 by Crossway, a publishing ministry of Good News Publishers. Used by permission. All rights reserved.

Scripture quotations marked NIV are taken from The Holy Bible, New International Version® NIV® Copyright © 1973 1978 1984 2011 by Biblica, Inc.™ Used by permission. All rights reserved worldwide.

Scripture quotations marked NRSV are from the New Revised Standard Version Bible, copyright © 1989 National Council of the Churches of Christ in the United States of America. Used by permission. All rights reserved worldwide.

Scripture quotations marked RSV are from the Revised Standard Version of the Bible, copyright © 1946, 1952, and 1971 National Council of the Churches of Christ in the United States of America. Used by permission. All rights reserved worldwide.

Scripture quotations marked TLB are taken from The Living Bible copyright © 1971. Used by permission of Tyndale House Publishers, Inc., Carol Stream, Illinois 60188. All rights reserved.

Excerpt from TUESDAYS WITH MORRIE: AN OLD MAN, A YOUNG MAN AND LIFE'S GREATEST LESSON by Mitch Albom, copyright © 1997 by Mitch Albom. Used by permission of Doubleday, an imprint of the Knopf Doubleday Publishing Group, a division of Penguin Random House LLC. All rights reserved.

Some content taken from THE WOUNDED HEART, by Dan B. Allender. Copyright © 1990, 1995, 2008. by permission of NavPress. All rights reserved. Represented by Tyndale House Publishers, Inc.

Some content taken from THE CRY OF THE SOUL, by Dan B. Allender and Tremper Longman, III. Copyright © 1994. Used by permission of NavPress. All rights reserved. Represented by Tyndale House Publishers, Inc.

Excerpt taken from My Utmost for His Highest by Oswald Chambers, © 1935 by Dodd Mead & Co., renewed © 1963 by the Oswald Chambers Publications Assn., Ltd. Used by permission of Discovery House Publishers, Grand Rapids MI 49501. All rights reserved.

Excerpt from THE SCREWTAPE LETTERS by CS LEWIS © copyright CS Lewis Pte Ltd 1942. Used with permission.

Excerpt from THE PATH OF WAITING by Henri Nouwen Copyright © Henri Nouwen (Crossroad, 1995). Reprinted by arrangement with The Crossroad Publishing Company. www.crossroadpublishing.com.

Quotes from pp. 154-55, 232-33 from THE DIVINE CONSPIRACY by DALLAS WILLARD Copyright © 1998 by Dallas Willard. Reprinted by permission of HarperCollins Publishers.

Cover design: Cindy Kiple

Interior design: Audra Nelessen

Back cover author photo: Jill Fager

ISBN 978-1-0772-6266-9

Printed in the United States of America.

July 2019

A Mission Central resource

missioncentral.church

For Trevor and Bonnie

Contents

Introduction ix

PART ONE: LAWS TO BREAK
CHAPTER 1 Get Things Done 3
CHAPTER 2 Follow the Plan 15

PART TWO: PRACTICES FOR LIFE
CHAPTER 3 Feeling 27
CHAPTER 4 Giving and Receiving Attention 55
CHAPTER 5 Asking for Help 77
CHAPTER 6 Waiting 95

Conclusion 111
Acknowledgements 115
Notes 117

Introduction

As I squeezed out another glop of blue paint onto my palette, I glanced again at the pond. It was stitched over with green in unexpected places, and I hoped I could capture that, but I was struggling with a cheap brush and an eight-by-ten-inch canvas. I certainly was no painter to speak of. On the way down to this little retreat week in Indiana with my wife Katie, I had bought some basic supplies on a whim. My mother is a painter, so I figured it couldn't hurt to give it a shot. But the colorful oval in my painting only bore a passing resemblance to the gorgeous, sun-grooved body of water I was looking at. I struggled to get the shape of the black fence along the border right, and the leaves of the trees in the distance came out blotchy.

The painting wasn't the only thing I was working on that week. Katie and I were in Indiana not merely to take a break, but also to take stock of our lives. Katie was only a few months out of rehab for an eating disorder, and in the intervening months, I had run myself ragged between the demands of work and school. Rest, reprieve, and refuge were long overdue. We walked through the woods and rowed across the pond. We looked up at the star-speckled canopy and breathed clean air. Katie ate well. I painted.

As I painted, my mind wandered over the preceding months. I began to ask questions about the patterns that I had seen and felt at work, in my studies, and in our marriage. Why was I always so driven to succeed, even when success led to strife and exhaustion? I yearned deeply for something different. I wanted to be a whole person, alive to God and others. But somewhere along the way, things had gotten out of whack in my soul. Rest, peace, patience, and love seemed more elusive than ever, even while I pursued a seminary degree and worked at a church. You'd have thought I had all the advantages: a loving family, supportive co-workers, attentive pastors, faithful friends. If anyone was set up to live a life of Christian vitality and joy, it was me. But something had muddied the waters.

A few weeks earlier, my pastor friend Trevor had confronted me about this muddy quality of my soul, and I was still coming to terms with his words. I had not expected to hear something like that from him. In fact, I had only met with him to try and convince him to give me a job. I was then on staff in an administrative role at my home church. But I wanted more elbow room in order to do hands-on, face-to-face ministry. My church was nestled into the largely white, tidy suburb of Wheaton, Illinois, but Trevor had recently planted a church in the much more diverse city of Aurora. I wanted to build relationships with Christians from different racial and cultural backgrounds, and I knew Trevor would be a great leader to follow.

But Trevor was not concerned about whether I might make a good addition to his team. He was concerned about me and Katie. He asked me questions like,

"It's only been two years since you graduated from college, right?"

"What if God is doing something in you through this admin work, even though you don't always like it?"

"How is Katie's health?"

"Why not wait?"

Trevor's questions drew my attention to the things that mattered most: care for my soul before God, and care for Katie. I felt caught off guard as I realized how unsatisfactory my answers were. ("Why not wait?" Because I don't want to!) As Trevor listened, he warned me of a pattern he discerned: "In the face of life's challenges, people respond in many ways. We can fall into unhealthy patterns in order to cope. Some people develop an anxiety disorder. Some people develop an eating disorder. And some people develop a ministry disorder."

I was surprised by how clear that diagnosis sounded as soon as Trevor said the words. A ministry disorder. I knew in the deep places of my being that these were words of healing, as much as they hurt to hear. As the Scriptures say, "Faithful are the wounds of a friend" (Proverbs 27:6).

The phrase "ministry disorder" captured so much of what I had struggled with up to that point, and the shape of my fears and failures even today. Things were out of order in my soul, and in the way that I did the work of ministry. Instead of drawing strength from prayer and marriage to serve and minister to others, I was caught up in endless ministry responsibilities while my personal walk with God and with Katie languished. I wasn't directing my gaze toward God, looking for his mercy and love; I was always looking for how to get ahead, to stay on top, to get things done. When Trevor said those words, I knew things needed to change. But how did things get so out of hand to begin with?

As I painted that pond in Indiana, I started looking for answers to that question. In the months since, I've spent time looking at my childhood and adolescence, trying to understand how patterns that developed early on still influence how I think, feel, and act. Conversations with Katie, with friends and family, and with pastors and counselors have helped me identify these patterns. Looking into my own heart to try to understand it has been both painful and at times confusing. Like the prophet Jeremiah, I've often feel like saying, "The heart is deceitful above all things, and desperately sick; who can understand it?" (Jeremiah 17:9 ESV). Yet God has been gracious, and has given me merciful moments of clarity. I'm still learning about who I am, and who I can become by God's grace. What I've found so far has helped me take steps toward a fuller, more joyful life. The better I understand myself, the better I'm able to live life as a gift to those around me.

We read in the Bible that "the kingdom of God is . . . righteousness and peace and joy in the Holy Spirit" (Romans 14:17 RSV). We are meant to abound in spiritual goodness that extends to everyone around us. Jesus said that everyone who believes in him will have rivers of living water flowing out from their heart (John 7:38). In Christ, our very person can become a source of refreshment and blessing for others. Yet as I've looked at my life—my tendency to over-work, my willingness to put marriage second to a ministry career, my need for control—I've seen that the rivers of my soul have become clogged up with mud and debris. In the process, God has brought something unexpected to my attention: my attempts to be a good Christian often get in the way of living his kind of life. You might think that we should always try as hard as we can to be the best Christians we can be. But for me, "being a good Christian" has become a project that, over time, has had less and less to do with the Holy Spirit's real work in me, and has generated more and more muck in the rivers of life.

This "good Christian" project is largely social. At least in Christian communities, being a good Christian can be socially rewarding. Christian community is, rightly, focused on the formation of a certain kind of life. But the exterior features of that life—the cultural quirks, language, and relevant information—are much easier to learn than the interior features of peace, joy, and love. And I've always had the external features down pat. I've known the Scriptures since childhood, and a good chunk of church tradition to boot. I've been involved in my church for as long as I can remember. I've led ministry activities with aplomb. I've been the poster child, the golden boy, the "kind of person who makes it all worth it" for my teachers and pastors. You know the type.

But in addition to the social reward of enjoying that "golden boy" status, I have internalized a system of expectations and achievement that come with the project. Doing the things that good Christians do has become a modus operandi, a deeply-ingrained set of habits. It is not just a way of impressing other people, it is a way of regulating my total experience. If I keep it up, I tell myself, things will work out all right for me. Along the way, I don't look for pity, or mercy, or help. I can manage the project myself.

But, for all its squeaky clean, shiny gleam, this way of life has failed me. As it turns out, "being a good Christian" in this way doesn't leave much room for being a humble Christian when I'm wrong, being an honest Christian about my weaknesses, or being a healthy Christian when I experience negative emotions. It leaves me pretending I'm holier than I am, because honest confession of my flaws is too painful. It blinds me to my own complex feelings, because I want to believe I'm just a happy person. Worst of all, it makes a spirit of contempt grow within my heart toward those who don't measure up. When I see the shortcomings of brothers and sisters in Christ, it's so easy for me to decide that they are bad Christians. In the end, it locks me within the small room of my own pride, detached from the world of people around me, unable to genuinely celebrate or love others. As it stands, being a good Christian is making me a bad human being.

Jesus once told a story about this kind of dynamic. Today, we could call it "The Story of the Good Christian and the Bad Christian." It goes like this:

"Two men went up to the temple to pray, one a Pharisee and the other a tax collector. The Pharisee stood by himself and prayed: 'God, I thank you that I am not like other people—robbers, evildoers, adulterers—or even like this tax collector. I fast twice a week and give a tenth of all I get.' But the tax collector stood at a distance. He would not even look up to heaven, but beat his breast and said, 'God, have mercy on me, a sinner.'" (Luke 18:10-13 NIV).

It's a simple story. Jesus doesn't embellish it with detail or give a lengthy explanation like he does for some of his other parables. He just says, "I tell you that this man [the tax collector], rather than the other, went home justified before God. For all those who exalt themselves will be humbled, and those who humble themselves will be exalted" (Luke 18:14 NIV).

It's sobering that the one who "exalted himself" was not up to anything "bad." He was being a good Jew. He was doing church things, practicing important spiritual disciplines meant to draw him close to God. Even so, his prayer is not really about God. It's about how well he measures up. The tax collector takes the opposite approach. He puts himself low enough, acknowledging his need, that God can raise him up. He knows he needs to receive mercy, so he can.

I want that kind of mercy. I want to be able to pray, "God, have mercy on me, a sinner." And learning to pray that prayer means unlearning the things that keep me from praying it: the different ways that I've tried to measure up, to hold it together, and to prove I'm not a bad Christian. I've come to see two specific patterns that have functioned as the unstated laws of "being a good Christian" in my life:

1. Get Things Done
2. Follow the Plan

In the first section of the book, I'll share a little about each of these laws, how I learned to follow it, and how it's contributed to my ministry disorder. As much as I still feel the weight of these laws, I'm finding that loving God and loving other people requires me to let go of the sense of stability and control that they give me. So in this season, I'm beginning to let them slide off my shoulders. I'm unlearning them. As I do, I find I finally have room to take up the "easy yoke" of Jesus (Matthew 11:30).

And that yoke fits perfectly. Jesus never puts a burden on me that's too hard to bear. His expectations never bend my soul out of shape. Instead, he calls forth the best of who I am, making my rivers run clean and bright again. He makes me want to live into that "righteousness and peace and joy in the Holy Spirit." And he makes me believe doing so is possible.

As I let go of being a good Christian and lean into the care of Jesus, I've discovered a few things that I can do to cooperate with God's work in my heart. In the second part of this book, I'll share about four such practices:

1. Feeling
2. Giving and Receiving Attention
3. Asking for Help
4. Waiting

These are practices that are available to anyone, at any time in their life. They do not require special expertise, just a heart willing to learn. While they aren't the usual activities you would find on a list of spiritual disciplines, I've discovered that they work in much the same way that traditional practices like Bible-reading, prayer, and confession do: as I do my part (which is really not that difficult) God faithfully shows up to do his, using the experience to refashion the spaces in my soul that need some work.

For me, my marriage with Katie has been the primary impetus and catalyst for change in my life as I learn how to be a bad Christian. Not because our marriage has been particularly holy, but because it has forced me to face up to my limits and weaknesses. About two years into our marriage, Katie experienced a mental and physical health crisis which in turn became a painful and sobering marriage crisis as it collided with my ministry disorder. The lessons that this book tries to communicate emerged directly from the hard work we each had to do in that season, by ourselves and together. This is not a marriage book, and the ideas in it are relevant to those who are married or unmarried. Even so, our marriage has been for me (to shift metaphors) both the garden where God is working on my soul and the spade he uses to do the work. So, I'll incorporate some of our story in each chapter as it relates to the ideas at hand.

When Katie and I left our retreat in Indiana, we so wanted to return. We had tasted grace. We had enjoyed goodness. We had known the generosity of God's presence in the woods and water, and in feeling the weight of things lift, if just a little, from our shoulders. I put my painting of the pond on a bookshelf at home, and have carried it into my days in the back of my mind since then. It reminds me of what the Christian life is meant to be about: letting God's life flow through us.

If you struggle with being a good Christian, I hope that in some small but significant way this book can help. Our life with God is not meant to be a project we manage to keep the chaos of life at bay. It is not about following laws so that we can measure up. Letting God's life flow through us means giving up on that project. It means unlearning the rules that draw us away from the internal work of the Spirit, even if they help us keep up external appearances. It means caring more about love than reputation, and more about simple spiritual substance than social status. It means believing that the love of God is so good that it's worth unclenching our hands to open them up to him.

If you've felt the burden of trying to be a good Christian, I hope that this book can help you learn how to be a bad one, too.

PART ONE

LAWS TO BREAK

CHAPTER 1
GET THINGS DONE

In the 1994 film Forrest Gump, the much-beloved title character enlists to serve in Vietnam just after graduating from college. Forrest, who would go on to win the Medal of Honor, shares his simple attitude about life at boot camp: "Now for some reason I fit in the Army like one of them round pegs. It's not really hard. You just make your bed real neat and remember to stand up straight and always answer every question with, 'Yes, Drill Sergeant!'"

What was true for Forrest about the Army has been true for me about school throughout my life: I just fit like one of them round pegs. On the first day of kindergarten, I was already impatient for things to start. I said goodbye to my mom, who had driven me to school, and excitedly ran to the front door. Several other first-day kindergarteners were there, and their mothers had actually parked and were waiting with them until the school day started. I remember thinking, "What are all these moms doing here? This is school; no need for moms!"

Once the doors opened, the experience of school did not disappoint my eager expectations. There were a bunch of kids my age I could meet, even if some of them seemed kind of shy and needed their moms before the school day started. I also discovered these kind, affectionate adults called teachers who organized activities for us, including playtime and a nap. Besides that, it turned out that we got to learn things all day! What could be better than that? I was hooked.

It wasn't long before the love of learning merged with another powerful drive: the love of getting things done. The first take-home worksheet I ever received was a math assignment. I don't remember any of the details about the assignment itself, but I do remember that as soon as I got home from school, I went to Dad's big desk in our living room, pulled the worksheet out of my backpack, and finished it in its entirety before moving on to playtime. I did not ask Mom for help. Standing at a couple of decades' remove from this event, I'm struck by how odd my behavior was for an elementary school student. Most students still need someone to remind them to get their homework done even into high school. Somehow, I had already developed an abnormal conscientiousness. I had decided that whatever I needed to do, I would get it done.

So it was that "Get Things Done" became one of the unwritten laws of my life. Following this law served me well, especially as a student. The intellectual curiosity that made me love kindergarten continued to flourish, and I soaked up new information and skills like a Bounty paper towel. I took to writing in particular, and found joy in putting words together. Like many "round-peg" students who have an easy time focusing, remembering details, and following technical instructions, I was consistently rewarded with teachers' appreciation and good grades. At the same time, my focus came to rest on these rewards, often at the expense of other experiences. I was always ready to throw a classmate under the bus by tattling if it helped ingratiate me with a teacher, and found I had few friends as a result.

As a teenager, I realized that following this law could also open up opportunities beyond the classroom. Rather than just completing assignments that my teachers were giving me, I could imagine my own projects and then accomplish them. Some of these were short-lived: I tried to start a student leadership group among my classmates that met all of one time. As I outgrew the tattling stage and learned how to build better friendships, I found ways to genuinely serve others. I started a small group with peers that met for several years, and a weekly summer discussion and prayer night the summer before my senior year. It was so gratifying to see a need, imagine a way to address it, and then see that imagined project come to life. I came to see that my particular knack for productivity was a gift from God. Getting things done became a way to love other people.

This penchant for productivity has opened up further vistas in adult life. Shortly after finishing college, I began a full-time administrative position at my local church, overseeing several of our ministry teams. I found I could organize dozens of people on joint projects, helping everyone stay on track to see beautiful services of worship come together each week. Other leaders could count on me to take care of the details, and that trust felt ennobling and exciting. I may or may not have heard the phrase "well-oiled machine" used to describe the ministries I led. But more than the sense of order, I was encouraged by the knowledge that team members were enjoying the work, serving God and his people on healthy teams. That experience delighted me and validated my administrative gifts.

For all its advantages, though, living by the law of getting things done has also taken its toll. It has served me so well, opened so many doors, and led to so much success that I have come to deeply fear what I would do without it. What if I couldn't get things done? Being capable in any situation has become a core aspect of my sense of identity. I'm afraid that, if I couldn't get things done, I wouldn't be me anymore. Behind much of my productivity is not a pure desire to love God and others, but a desperate bid for self-protection. My sense of well-being depends on maintaining my edge. It feels like if I don't get things done, the world will fall apart. Or at least I will.

A Western Law

I have a sense that I'm not the only one who feels bound to the law of getting things done. Contemporary work culture in much of the Western world fosters it. I remember interviewing for a job once and hearing, "We do value work-life balance, but when the chips are down we expect you to be all in." I think this was code for, "We like to say we value work-life balance, but actually we don't. We value getting things done." Gallup reports that the average work week for a full-time employee in the United States is forty-seven hours, with almost one in five workers putting in sixty hours or more. Research from the Harvard Business Review shows that Dutch workaholics (defined as those with "a compulsion to work" who have trouble detaching from work even at home) "reported more health complaints . . . they also reported a higher need for recovery, more sleep problems, more cynicism, more emotional exhaustion, and more depressive feelings" than other workers. Many of us have formed a relationship with getting things done that is wearing away at our bodies and minds.

A classmate of mine once reflected on the ubiquity of coffee, "What does it say about our society that the average worker relies on a chemical stimulant to function in the average work environment?" This question has stayed with me over the years. The health hazards or benefits of caffeine continue to be debated, but I'm struck by how easily we normalize staying up late and waking up early, pushing beyond our physical limits. We might ask a corresponding question, "What does it say about God's expectations for our lives that he designed us to spend about one third of them unconscious?" If someone invented a button we could simply press and not need to sleep at all, I can guess how popular it would be. But God built the need for sleep into us. It's as though he is saying, "There's more to life than getting things done."

I want to listen to that voice that tells me there's more to life than this law. But so often, it doesn't feel safe not to get things done. Doing whatever I feel responsible to do crowds out all other priorities. Tending to my soul, spending time with friends and family, enjoying life—none of these are sacred. I have shown myself willing to sacrifice any and all of them for the sake of getting things done. Those sacrifices follow certain patterns that arise as I struggle to get ahead. Exploring each of these patterns in turn shows just how cramped and diminished my life can become under this law.

The Need for External Validation

One pattern that emerged early on was my need for external validation. At school, I soon discovered the thrill of grades. It felt so good to get that letter or number at the top of an assignment that meant, "Great job." In third grade, we received a quarterly report card with four options for each subject: Excellent, Good, Satisfactory, and Unsatisfactory. When my first report card for the year came in, I saw that my teacher Miss Bertsche had given me either Excellent or Good for everything except handwriting, which she marked as Satisfactory.

Now to understand the emotional effect this grade had on me, you need to know something about Miss Bertsche. Imagine the most kind, competent, affectionate, and patient teacher you can: the kind of teacher about whom John Steinbeck once wrote, "She left her signature on us . . . I suppose that to a large extent I am the unsigned manuscript of that [teacher]. What deathless power lies in the hands of such a person." I knew that Miss Bertsche cared about me and loved me.

For all that, I took offense at her evaluation of my penmanship: Handwriting isn't even a real subject! Who cares if my letters are a little sloppy? You know who cares? Miss Bertsche cares. Well, am I going to show her! I'll give her the most beautiful handwriting she's ever seen. I'll bamboozle her with the elegance of my cursive script, the precision of the way I cross my t's. I will achieve mastery! I will be Excellent!

And that's just what I did. When the next report card rolled in, I got top marks in handwriting. So there, Miss Bertsche, I thought.

This kind of competitive, eager drive for grades often came to displace concern for real learning, and sometimes set me at odds even with educators who had my best interests at heart. I'm embarrassed to admit that I was still largely working for the grades rather than the learning even into college. It wasn't until my Junior year as an undergrad that a professor challenged my thinking about grades and forced me to evaluate what I really cared about in my education. Because of this professor's influence, I started reading other professors' feedback to think about what they had to say and what I was learning, but if possible without looking at the number or letter grade. That habit remains tentative; even now as a seminary student, I've only willfully resisted nervously checking my grades online after I complete each assignment. But whenever I do, I find just a bit more freedom, remembering that I'm studying theology because I want to learn about God and love him better, not to get the grade.

Outside of class, I'm also tempted to look for external validation for the work I'm doing. I find myself prioritizing the things that are likely to affect my reputation, while neglecting equally important things that I can't put on a resume. Staying a little bit late at the office to answer email makes me look competent. The people getting those emails get to know that they can count on me. More hidden is the cost of the time I'm not spending loving people in less impressive ways, like giving my brother a call or remembering (for once) to write that birthday card for a friend.

Neglecting Relationships

I often choose to prioritize the things I "need" to get done over the people I love. The truth is, love and productivity are often in tension—I can keep working on a project, or I can wrap up for the day and pay attention to my friends and family. Love involves patterns of presence that can't really be called "getting things done": listening, sitting, experiencing beauty together. These are the kind of things which are not meant to "get done" but rather to be inhabited, even savored. It's true that getting things done is a way for me to love people, but it's not the only way. If I reduce love to getting things done, fun and spontaneity and joy begin to fade from my interactions with other people.

Katie suffers most from this pattern in my life. It's so easy for me to focus my efforts and conserve energy for work projects, while giving Katie what little emotional capacity I have left at the end of the day. The consequences of not doing well at work often feel more potent and scary than the consequences of giving Katie less than my best.

The year after I graduated from college, I was eager to finally do some exciting projects besides my schoolwork. I threw myself into getting all sorts of things done that I hadn't had time for in college. As I did, I didn't really pay attention to Katie's health, which had been deteriorating steadily.

Meanwhile, I was getting so much done! Here's what my average week looked like: I worked a full-time job at our church, Sunday to Thursday. Fridays I sometimes took off, but I used that time to meet with friends who I was mentoring. On Wednesday nights I was attending a Bible study at another church where I was trying to build relationships, and on Thursday nights I often attended (and sometimes preached at) the weekly gathering of a local post-prison ministry. On Saturdays I visited a refugee family in our community to help lead ESL lessons, and I was the refugee ministry coordinator for our whole church. To top it off, I also was taking an online seminary class, taking detailed notes on atonement theory and the dual nature of Christ in the wee hours of the morning and filling spare moments of each weekend with hastily drafted theological research.

Katie and I saw each other at suppertime a few nights a week and fit bits and snatches of conversation into my packed evenings. The nights that I was off at church activities, she was taking herself to one doctor after another. Sometimes I remembered to ask her how the appointments went; sometimes I didn't. Often a couple days would go by before we even had time to talk about what the doctor had said. She was also working her own demanding job as a nurse at a rehabilitation hospital. But when we did have time together, I would have so many things to verbally process from my ministry adventures that I didn't always get around to asking her about her day at work. Katie would eventually initiate much-needed change in this dynamic, but we'll return to that part of the story in chapter four.

An "Efficiency Bias"

Getting things done feels good, and getting things done quickly feels even better. So, I tend to spend my time doing things that I know I can get done quickly, or that I know will contribute to projects I'm working on. It's easy to justify this bias: I'm responsible to get these things done, aren't I? When someone calls me, for example, I have a choice whether I will answer the phone or not. Sometimes setting the boundary of not answering the phone is important to attend to other priorities. At other times, it really is the best and most loving thing to pick up the phone and pay attention to the person on the other end of the line. And there are certain people who, I know, will take up a good chunk of time if I answer the phone. They are not efficient phone callers. When I'm talking with such a person, sometimes I'm tempted to multi-task and start working on email while I half-listen to them. Even in social contexts when I'm not pressed for time, I sometimes try to extricate myself from conversations as quickly as possible, because I don't want to expend the emotional energy it takes to really engage with another human being and whatever it is they want to share with me.

For all my love of productivity, though, I know that half-listening to someone while multi-tasking doesn't amount to truly loving them. When I'm talking to someone else, I want them to pay attention to me. When I give someone else only the margins of my attention while trying to be efficient, I'm treating them like an object or a problem to overcome as they relate to my projects and responsibilities. I no longer see them as a person who deserves to be taken seriously for their own sake. I'm not obeying the teaching of Jesus, "Do to others as you would have them do to you" (Luke 6:31 NRSV). Christian thinker Read Schuchardt writes that "the opposite of love is not hatred; it is efficiency." My efficiency bias keeps me from what Schuchardt aptly calls "the slow, difficult work of embodying God's love, one embodied soul at a time." Often, loving people requires inefficiency.

Anxiety and Exhaustion

Perhaps the most obvious cost of following the law of getting things done is the anxiety and exhaustion I end up carrying in my body and my soul because of it. I've found that often when I wake up in the morning, the first thoughts that flood my consciousness are the day's tasks and responsibilities. I hop out of bed to get through my morning routine and rush off to one thing or the other, mentally problem-solving as I go. Without intending to, I develop a kind of emotional myopia; my to-dos remain in focus, while everything else is a blur.

Anxiety is often beyond our control. When we're in its grip, we can't just turn it off; it feels like that leaky faucet that, despite our best efforts, just won't quit dripping. At the same time, I know that I've formed habits that contribute to my anxiety. I remember watching the Super Bowl with Katie's family, but keeping my smartphone on me. I would check it every once in a while. An email came through with bad news about a project I'd been working on for weeks, and I spent the rest of the evening thinking about it while the football and commercials rolled along. Anxiety isn't always my fault, but failing to set a boundary with work and letting it leech the joy out of family time is on me.

Exhaustion functions in the same way. I don't want to go through life tired, but often I find that's what I'm doing. Staying up until two in the morning to finish a seminary assignment makes me feel like I'm in control of my academic life. My inattentiveness to others' feelings as I muddle through the following day doesn't affect my grade. I end up skipping other things, like prayer or journaling, that feel like they just take too much energy, even though these practices might help me find that spiritual rest I really need. It's so easy to make excuses. And it's true that I can't just "stop being tired." But I can arrange my life so that I get to bed earlier. And when I do, even when it means getting a little less done, I rarely regret it.

Unlearning this law has been painful for me. Getting things done delivers such a sense of security and power. Still, I'm convinced the struggle is worth it. As I realize more and more how much I've been obeying this law, I'm inspired with hope for the kind of life I could live without it. What if I could be present to my wife, no matter how busy life was? What if I could rest in God's provision, rather than feeling constant anxiety? What if I could do my work motivated by a desire to love and serve others, rather than by an aching need to protect and promote myself? That sounds like the kind of life I want to live.

Before talking about steps toward that kind of life, there's another law to deal with.

CHAPTER 2

FOLLOW THE PLAN

When President George W. Bush and most of Congress decided to send troops to Iraq in 2003, apprehension and fear ran high in the United States and around the world. Many people of many different political persuasions believed the intervention was necessary, but even those who objected were anxious to see what would happen with boots on the ground. Shortly before U.S. troops were to be deployed, I watched a television interview with a U.S. general in which he described the strategy of the operation. The first step of the plan, he said, was to win every battle.

That line has stayed with me over the years. I was so impressed by the confidence of such a plan. This general did not say, "We'll fight a battle and see how it goes." He had his course charted, from beginning to end, and felt he knew how to make it work at each step. Looking back on the events that unfolded in the following years in Iraq, we now know it was not so simple. Even the idea of defined battles and discrete enemy lines lost relevance as the conflict descended into a protracted and unconventional insurgency. To this day, Iraq is marked by profound turmoil and instability.

There's something inside me, though, that still loves that line. Win every battle. It conveys an ideal of order, predictability, structure, and success. It always feels so good to have a plan.

As with getting things done, "Follow the Plan" became a rule of my life when I was still quite young. In seventh grade, I joined a student leadership program in my church's youth ministry. The program involved meeting with a mentor once a month, as well as regular meetings with other student leaders at church. I realized that I would need to keep track of when these events were scheduled. I had noticed that my dad kept his appointments in a little pocket book, and I asked him what it was called. "It's called a planner," he said. A planner. What a great name. "Would you like me to get you one?" he asked. Would I ever.

I kept on using planners just like the one my dad bought me in seventh grade all the way through college. I still have some of them among my keepsakes, for entertainment value. Here's a selection from the planner I used as a junior in high school:Scribbled in the margin of the front page:

Pizza Now 1-630-260-2161
Sunday January 25: Coord[inate] 2nd Service [at church]
Saturday February 7: ACT @ 8am Glenbard North (Bring ID)
Sunday March 22: 10am Coord. 2nd Service / 1:30-4:30pm Coordinators & Team Leaders Holy Week Mtng (Bring info)

Saturday June 6: 8:15am WA Graduation / Help Paige move / 4-7: Erik Nelson's Open House? / 6pm Katy Carlson Graduation Party
Friday July 24: 9:30-10:30 get rid of wisdom teeth

Having a planner gave me a sense of power. Armed with the details I recorded on a daily basis, I was confident that I wouldn't forget a meeting, miss a deadline, or fail to fulfill any of my many responsibilities. It also gave me a sense of stability. Time did not stretch out before me as an intimidating void, full of danger and unforeseeable twists of fate. Instead, it was divided up into neat little chunks, a day at a time, with straight lines. A whole year could fit in my pocket. If I wanted to know what would happen next, I just had to look ahead and see what I had written.

Sometimes I decided to look rather far ahead, and made plans well in advance. When I was about ten years old, my senior pastor mentioned one day that he didn't know Spanish, and that sometimes made it difficult to communicate with a Spanish-speaking pastor he knew. I knew that in junior high and high school, I would have a chance to study a foreign language. "I better learn Spanish," I decided as my pastor spoke, "so that I can talk to Spanish-speakers in our area with ease." Three years later, that's just what I did.

Another time, in junior high, a college student told me she had taken a gap year to Mexico and really benefited from the cross-cultural experience. It also improved her Spanish. "I better take a gap year to somewhere in Latin America," I decided as she spoke, "so that I can benefit from the cross-cultural experience and improve my Spanish." After graduating from high school, that's just what I did.

Just like with the law of getting things done, following the plan has worked to my advantage in many areas of life. It's often given me a sense of purpose and motivation. I rarely feel aimless, because I almost always have a plan to follow. The plan gives me a frame of reference that simplifies decisions. Great good can come from following good plans. I'm glad that I studied Spanish and took a gap year. (I'm glad that I got rid of my wisdom teeth, too!) Many wonderful experiences require planning, and I'm happy that many of my plans have turned out well.

At the same time, following the plan can also shield me from the sense of my own weakness. Plans are about controlling outcomes, and when my well-laid preparations succeed, I can so easily believe that I am in control of reality. It becomes part of my self-image as a good Christian who can get good things done, guaranteed. It's humbling to realize that the plans that have gone well in my life probably have more to do with God graciously blessing me than with how good at planning I am. And that illusion of control fades away quickly when plans don't succeed. In spite of my best efforts, life does not always fit itself into the timeline that I project in my planner. And coming up against those unplanned moments has forced me to see the ways in which following the plan can warp and limit my life.

One of these moments came on my gap year, which I spent in Peru. I had decided on Peru because a friend of a friend had a connection with some churches there in my denomination. With the help of a missions agency, I was able to line up a ministry internship from afar, including a family with whom I could live. I was told I'd be living with a Peruvian pastor, his British missionary wife, and their three children, who were around my age. I was so excited to go. I was sure I would love getting to know these people, forming deep friendships, and doing hands-on ministry at church with them.

When I arrived at the home of the pastor and his wife, many things went just according to plan. They had a place for me to stay, and helped me learn how to get around town. I quickly picked up responsibilities at their church. At the same time, something was off. The parents didn't really talk with their three children very much, and when they did, they were usually fighting. Mom always seemed to have someone or something to criticize, and Dad was having trouble getting along with his fellow pastors. "Well, we'll see how it goes," I thought. "Maybe they're having a bad couple of weeks." By the time I'd been in the country a month, though, it was clear to me that I had walked into an emotionally toxic and dysfunctional home. Mom and Dad could not reconcile their Christian idealism with how disillusioned all of their kids were with the church. They didn't have the emotional capacity to meet me where I was at in my first extended cross-cultural experience. Things were not going according to plan.

I felt stuck. What was I supposed to do? I considered whether it would be wise to pack up and just head home, but friends and family members had given money so that I could have this experience. I didn't want to bail. At the same time, I could feel myself shutting down. Without any close and safe relationships, I had trouble making sense of my place in Peru. Home didn't feel like home, not just because I was crossing cultures, but because I found myself caught in the middle of a slowly disintegrating family unit. I felt depressed. I found it unusually difficult to connect with other people. My energy levels slowed from full blast down to a drip.

The only thing I had left was the to-do list of ministry responsibilities. So, that's what I gave myself to. I followed the plan. The emotions I was experiencing were so bewildering that I did my best to set them aside and focus on the task at hand. By God's grace, the work I was involved with did prove fruitful. I learned more Spanish, volunteered at an after-school program, and helped out around the church as best I could. I was able to forge meaningful relationships with a handful of people. But even in those friendships, I didn't really share much of my anxiety and sadness, or the sense of listless wandering that characterized my day-to-day experience. I couldn't really share it, because I didn't know how to experience it in a meaningful way myself. It wasn't part of the plan.

In the middle of this emotional morass, another unexpected turn of events was developing. The first Sunday evening I was in Peru, Katie, who was by this time a close friend, happened to be available to Skype. We talked for quite some time about the country and my experiences so far, and what things were like as she began her senior year of high school. We agreed to Skype again the following week. And the week after that. In the days between our talks, as I reflected on our friendship, I realized what many of our mutual friends later told us had been obvious for months: I liked this woman! She was intelligent, perceptive, kind, beautiful, and (best of all) she liked talking with me. So, despite being over three thousand miles away and eight months from my return home, on the fourth Sunday, I shared my feelings with Katie. We began "dating" via Skype, still just once a week, until I returned home. We fell in love. That wasn't part of my gap year plan either.

As the beauty of my marriage with Katie has proved, great good can come from not following the plan. But I still find plans so attractive. They promise so much: predictability, stability, and results.

The thing about plans is that they tend to focus on tasks: what to do, how to accomplish a goal. Plans clear away emotional complexity and perplexing questions. But real life puts the emotional complexity and perplexing questions right back in. What I experienced in Peru had a totally different quality than the items on my to-do list. Depression does not follow the timeline in my planner.

I can't schedule falling in love like a dental appointment. Positive or negative, my feelings are not always linear and predictable. If I pay attention to my internal experience, it isn't divided up into neat little chunks, a day at a time, with straight lines.

Still, I follow the plan because I often feel like I don't have another option. It's how I navigate my life and maintain some sense of control in an uncontrollable world. I take care to follow the plan, because I believe it will take care of me. The Bible has a word for this kind of basic, all-encompassing attachment: worship. When there is something that I feel I cannot do without, that becomes my source of provision and well-being, then that thing is what I worship. That is how worship works. We worship what we believe will give us life, and we do what it says. The Bible uses the word "serve" as a synonym for worship in many contexts, specifically when it talks about worshipping God or worshipping idols:

> *Then the Israelites did evil in the eyes of the L*ORD *and served the Baals* JUDGES 2:11 NIV
>
> *The Israelites did evil in the eyes of the L*ORD*; they forgot the L*ORD *their God and served the Baals and the Asherahs* JUDGES 3:7 NIV
>
> *So the Israelites put away their Baals and Ashtoreths, and served the L*ORD *only* 1 SAMUEL 7:4 NIV

When I follow one of my laws, I do not feel the freedom to say no. I have to get everything done; I have to follow the plan. So, I serve the laws. I follow the plan, anxiously hoping that it will give me life—that my efforts to prepare for all eventualities will pay off in freedom from unexpected pain. I want the plan to provide me with what I need and protect me from what I fear. And because I'm the one that makes the plan, that's another way of saying that I try to provide for and protect myself. I step into the place that God wants to have in my life.

David writes, "The LORD is my shepherd; I shall not want. He makes me lie down in green pastures" (Psalm 23:1-2). When I let following the plan become an idol that I worship, it means that I spend my time and energy hunting down green pastures for myself, because I don't trust that God will come through for me. Pastor and author Pete Scazzero describes this dynamic as "that driving, grasping, fearful self-will that must produce, that must make something happen, that must get it done for God (just in case he doesn't)." Living by the plan crowds out God.

And as faithfully as I follow the plan, as rigorously as I obey the law of getting things done, as hard as I work at being a good Christian, it never seems like I can work hard enough. That's the problem with worshipping idols: they can't actually give us life like God can. Serving them inevitably warps and diminishes us, rather than making us the fuller and better people we long to be.

When we turn our hearts to God in worship, he gives us his life. And that experience is more like the surprise of my relationship with Katie than like a plan going off without a hitch. We don't connect with God like we do with a checklist; we connect with him like we do with a person. He invites us to put our faith in him and walk with him, which means receiving and relying on his love even when we don't know what's coming next.

For me, it's taken a few of my plans crashing and burning for me to start looking to God for that kind of provision and protection. I'll explore some of those fruitful failures in the chapters ahead. They've helped me see that I can't anticipate all eventualities, I can't shield myself from suffering, and life cannot fit in my planner. But it doesn't have to. I don't need to plan everything, because God will be with me even if there is pain, and he loves me so much he'll even provide blessings that I didn't strategize for. Life can be an adventure when it's not all plotted out, full of mystery and joyful discovery. God's plan, it turns out, is often better than mine.

Learning to see life that way has taken time, and effort, and more than a few tears, and I'm not done learning yet. But along the way, I've found a few practices that have helped me let go of my need to serve my idols.

PART TWO

PRACTICES FOR LIFE

CHAPTER 3

FEELING

EVERY YEAR GROWING UP, my family would take each summer to visit our relatives in Seattle. For my brother Benjamin and me, the whole point of the trip was to see our cousins Katherine, Alison, Anna, and Joseph. The six of us shared the joy of freewheeling playtimes and antics of all kinds. Each year, we would write and perform a miniature play for our aunts and uncles. It gave us all a chance to be dramatic and adventurous, slaying dragons and liberating kingdoms within the confines of a suburban living room. As we got older, childlike play gave way to adolescent conversation and the wonder of growing up together. The warm weight of twenty of these summer trips has settled in our souls; play, imagination, and recreation have led to great joy and love.

Our mutual trust has allowed us to be present to each other in grief, too. We were together the week after Grandpa died, and again five years later when Grandma died, too. We have had each other's backs through the ups and downs of both teenage and twenty-something social drama and heartbreak. We have come to know, as you may too, that the closest friends are those who can be with you not only in good times, but also in bad.

The meaning of any kind of intimate relationship is bound up with our emotional experience. So, it stands to reason that feelings would matter a great deal in our life with God.

This may seem like an obvious point, but the connection between my emotional life and my spiritual life came to me as a surprise. As a teenager, I had everything going for me to help me make this connection. My mom was a counselor, and I grew up in a church community focused on prayer for emotional healing. It was not unusual for people, upon visiting our church for the first time, to be moved by something in the service and spontaneously burst into tears. Our pastor counseled these folks, "Pay attention to what makes you cry. God may be telling you something." Because of my mom's work, I didn't buy into the stigma that still sometimes lingers around psychology and therapy in the popular imagination. I knew that emotions were important, and that paying attention to your feelings was a good thing.

I just didn't think I needed to worry about that sort of thing myself. I was a joyful, confident guy. When I came to church, I didn't cry; I was happy. My attitude was that healing prayer and counseling are wonderful for the poor souls who needed it. But I was a good Christian! I was really thankful that our church was a safe place for broken people, but I figured I was mostly put together. After all, I had the benefit of growing up in such an emotionally sensitive community. I must have dodged all the issues that led other people to need healing in the first place. I assumed that, because I was a basically happy person, I must be pretty emotionally healthy, without the same need for support and healing as the "broken" people at church. In reality, I was simply enjoying extended emotional positivity in a relatively care-free life. I had no inkling that experiencing sadness, anger, and fear was on the horizon, nor that those experiences could shape me in good and meaningful ways.

Because I had bracketed off emotional concerns as something largely relevant to people less happy than myself, I didn't really think about my emotional life when I thought about my relationship with God. My thoughts about spirituality tended toward what I was doing, not what I was feeling. As always, I wanted to follow the plan and to get things done. In my walk with God, that consisted of traditional practices like reading the Bible, fasting, and praying. Our church placed a strong emphasis on confession of sin, so I also tried to do that regularly in a small group. I had a strong bent toward theology, so I did my best to understand the things of God, and then do them correctly. In my mind, it was paramount to think and do the right thing, regardless of how I was feeling.

Then I moved to Peru. As I described in chapter two, it gradually dawned on me that I was residing in an emotionally dysfunctional home. I had no idea what to do with my own negative emotions. Anxiety, sadness, anger, depression: this was all virgin territory, as unfamiliar to me as the mountains and abandoned Incan cities on the horizon. Why didn't I feel good anymore? Why couldn't I seem to muster the energy to "get past" the difficulty of my situation and still enjoy God's goodness?

I didn't find good answers to those questions while I was in Peru. But I now see my time there as a turning point, because it was when I first began to grapple with negative emotions in a significant way. Even if, at the time, I didn't know how to make room for those feelings, I was entering into a new phase of life. As a child, I had been sheltered, but now as an adult I would enter into a life of both joy and pain. And, much to my surprise, I would find God just as much in the pain as in the joy.

Finding God in Sadness

Finding God in positive emotions is relatively easy. We can just give thanks to God for what we're happy about! As James writes, "Is anyone happy? Let them sing songs of praise" (5:13 NIV). That kind of emotional connection to God was familiar to me even before my time in Peru. Yet when I began to experience negative emotions more intensely in Peru, God often seemed absent. My sense of listlessness left me feeling distant from God more often than not.

Whenever it surfaced, this sense of distance distressed me, and it drove me to prayer. I really wanted to make it go away, to somehow return to positive feelings. So I would pray, remind myself of the truths of Scripture, confess my sin, and work hard. I did my best not to focus on the negative feelings, and instead tried to "stay positive." For all my efforts, though, disappointment and anger kept bubbling up at inopportune times. My incapacity to reconcile myself to the challenges of my situation and the feelings they stirred up in me left me feeling divided from myself, confused, and bitter. Negative emotions were just that, a negative experience. I couldn't find any more meaning than that in them.

But another opportunity to return to this same set of feelings came to me a few years later. Katie's health issues had reached a crisis point, and I was exhausted. I spoke with one of our pastors, and she encouraged me to see a counselor. I was experiencing so much pain at the time, the notion that maybe I was the kind of poor soul who needed counseling no longer seemed far-fetched. So, I decided to try it out. When I began meeting with my counselor, I thought we would talk about how to "deal with" sadness and anger; I wanted to learn how to make them go away so I could be happy again, to "get things done" emotionally. But my counselor instead wanted me to take time to "get to know" these negative feelings. He encouraged me to make room for each feeling, paying attention to it. Rather than running away into work or other distractions, I could "listen" to fear, to anger, and to sadness. Or so I was told!

So, I decided to try it out. When I noticed I was having a hard day, instead of venting about it in hopes of feeling better, I just "sat with it" for a while. I allowed myself to feel sad when sad things happened. If Katie came home with discouraging news from a doctor's appointment, I wouldn't immediately launch into a new task after talking with her. Instead, I would take a few minutes to journal and pray, noticing my responses. Paying attention to negative emotions wasn't a purely novel concept for me, but as I got counseling, it was the first time I really began to welcome these feelings instead of trying to "fix" them.

As I began to welcome negative emotions, nothing dramatic happened at first. I spent more time paying attention to how I was feeling, more time journaling, more time talking to Katie and to friends and others about my emotional experience. There was no noticeable change, just a growing familiarity with my feelings. Then one night, after a particularly discouraging day and an overwhelming fight with Katie, I found myself at the end of my rope. I felt immeasurably sad. I was finishing the day by reading a Psalm, and that day it happened to be Psalm 21, which begins, "O LORD, in your strength the king rejoices, and in your salvation how greatly he exults!" (ESV). I did not feel like rejoicing. But I did feel like I needed strength. The song "Please Be My Strength" by Michael Gungor came to mind. I decided to listen to it before continuing with my prayer time.

Please be my strength.
Please be my strength.
'Cause I don't have any more.
I don't have any more.

As I listened, I wrote, "Even as I'm listening, I find myself resisting it. I'm not that kind of Christian — weak, powerless. I mean, God helps them and that's beautiful, but I just don't need that kind of help. I'm good. I'm ashamed to need that kind of help." I wrote a few more words, and then I stopped, because something was happening to me. I was crying.

Tears can be a gift. That night, as I cried, I felt a closeness to the Lord in the middle of my sadness like I had not known before. It was the kind of closeness I had felt in the past when crying with someone safe, a feeling of being known and loved, and somehow helped even though nothing about the sad situation has changed. It was the gift of being weak, the gift of being a bad Christian. I did not measure up. I did not have it all together. And God was there, loving me. He was speaking to me through my tears: "I love you. I will always be here for you. I will always take care of you."

Somehow, my pain had become a place where I could experience God's love. It was as though I needed the warm-up of paying attention to my emotions more intentionally for a few months before it was even possible for me to experience something like that. As I got to know my emotions for myself, I now could share them with God. I could find God in the sadness.

This new awareness of sadness changed the way I pray. The experience of being with God in tears allowed me to talk with him about sadness and other difficult emotions more readily. For the first time, Scripture passages that gave voice to grief or anger also gave voice to my own heart. I recall one Wednesday morning, about a year later, when Katie and I were in a place of conflict and distance. I felt weak. The Psalm in my reading plan that day opened like this:

> *How long, O LORD? Will you forget me forever?*
> *How long will you hide your face from me?*
> *How long must I take counsel in my soul*
> *and have sorrow in my heart all the day?*
>
> PSALM 13:1-2 ESV

I wrote out the words in my journal and prayed them to the Lord. Although I was still in pain, I felt that he was listening, and that he cared for me and Katie. Even while the difficult situation was ongoing, even before I felt happy, I found that God was with me. I now knew that even in the depth of dark emotion, God would hold me fast. Sadness took on new meaning as it became an opportunity for connection with God. Pain was still painful, but it was no longer pointless. It was a place for the love of God.

Recognizing Anger and Shame

As this gradual process of emotional awareness continued, anger also came to my attention. Like many Christians, I grew up hearing the words of Jesus about anger:

> *"You have heard that it was said to those of ancient times, 'You shall not murder'; and 'whoever murders shall be liable to judgment.' But I say to you that if you are angry with a brother or sister, you will be liable to judgment; and if you insult a brother or sister, you will be liable to the council; and if you say, 'You fool,' you will be liable to the hell of fire."*
>
> MATTHEW 5:21-22 NRSV

Jesus does not mince his words. He takes anger as a matter of serious concern for those who would put his teachings into practice. Unfortunately, my take-away from this passage for many years was to treat it as a rule, another law to follow: don't get angry! Knowing this rule, of course, did not keep me from getting angry. Like anyone, I still experienced the surge of adrenaline that comes when I believe I've been mistreated. I still felt anger, but I also felt guilty about it. To avoid that guilt, I tried to minimize or rationalize my anger. Instead of saying, "I feel angry," I'd say, "I feel frustrated." If I could admit to myself that I was angry, I would try to "fix" it by arguing with myself about why I shouldn't feel angry.

In other words, trying hard not to be angry did not get me anywhere close to true freedom from anger. It just kept me from being honest with myself and others about how much anger I really felt. As best I can tell, I am not the only Christian who struggles with honesty about anger. I recall reading in one book, "Christians anger only rarely and only righteously." A statement like this makes me wonder if the writer has met many Christians! My anger, at least, came around a little more often than "rarely." Shortly after getting married, it began showing up unexpectedly and frequently, in ways that I felt powerless to manage.

Money was a particular flashpoint for me. Katie and I were both still in school, working part time. We didn't have a shoestring budget; we had about enough budget for a shoestring. To keep track of our income and spending, I constructed an unwieldy, multi-colored Excel spreadsheet into which we entered the details of our paystubs and receipts. Every few weeks, I would review the file, and I would notice some small detail that I believed Katie had entered inaccurately, such as a missing transaction or a number in the wrong column. Immediately, I would get Katie and go over the details with great agitation until I knew exactly what had happened. Then I would lecture her about how important it was to handle our money rightly. Needless to say, Katie felt overwhelmed and unloved during these fights.

From the outside, the unhealthy emotional dynamics may seem obvious. But from the inside, facing the stress of our financial situation each month, I felt like I "couldn't help" the anger. It just came automatically; the "don't get angry" rule did not provide a way out. Confronting Katie in anger when something "was wrong" was the only way I knew how to "solve the problem," whatever the problem was. In my mind, the anger was incidental. I was focused on getting things done and following the plan: fixing the spreadsheet, paying the bills, and making budget. I was blind to how much my anger was hurting Katie.

During one of our arguments, Katie confronted me by asking, "Why are you so upset?" I was taken aback. I figured it was obvious: "I'm upset because I care about using our money rightly, so that our lives are provided for." I paused for a few moments, grasping for a better explanation. "I'm upset because I care about you." Katie felt stung: "If it's because you care about me, then why are you so angry at me?" As our conversation continued, I had a (long-overdue) epiphany. In money matters, loving Katie doesn't just mean getting things done and following the plan. It also means communicating about money in a loving way, not in a condemning way. Katie cannot receive what I'm saying as a form of love if I say it with anger and judgment.

That conversation led me to try and understand where my anger about money was really coming from. Obviously, there are sometimes financial details that are important for me to discuss with Katie. But there is no reason for me to discuss them in anger and every reason to discuss them gently and graciously. So, why did I feel angry so suddenly at the smallest accounting inaccuracy? I remembered something that one of our pastors, who was also a licensed counselor, had said: even behind unhealthy anger, there is some kind of legitimate need. I came to see that my anger was not an appropriate response to something Katie had "done wrong"; it was an inappropriate response to my own deep needs. Specifically, I saw a relationship between my anger and a deep-seated need to be good.

In my mind, of course, being good meant getting things done and following the plan. With money, that meant paying the bills, limiting debt, and making our budget each month. Making a mistake with money was not just an oversight; to me, it felt unacceptable, irresponsible, and sinful. It felt like being a bad Christian. That's why my desire to be good ironically led to such an ungracious attitude toward Katie. In my mind, maintaining the Excel spreadsheet perfectly was my way of being good, of making sure I was never a bad Christian as far as money goes. When that standard of accounting felt threatened, I felt threatened, and I lashed out.

Another way of saying the same thing is that my anger was rooted in shame. I never thought of myself as someone who struggles with shame until Katie and I started seeing a counselor together. The idea of shame was not new to me; I had heard good preachers and teachers warning me about shame and self-condemnation for years. It was old news that it was possible for people to judge themselves in a way that's unhelpful, that everyone needs to look to the cross to receive God's grace and forgiveness. Preachers sometimes talked about the difference between conviction and shame. Conviction is a feeling of sorrow over what you've done wrong, which comes from the Holy Spirit and leads to confession, a sense of forgiveness, and joy. Shame is a sense of being wrong, which comes from the Enemy and leads to self-hatred, continual focus on oneself, and despair.

Because I understood these distinctions, I figured that shame and self-condemnation were not a significant part of my life. But as I talked about my experiences with our counselor, she seemed to think otherwise. One time, Katie and I were talking about a painful subject, and I started out speaking calmly, if sadly, and listening well. But then, while we continued to talk about some patterns in my behavior that were not helping our marriage, the conversation took a turn and I suddenly became overwhelmed and angry and began blaming Katie. In the moment, I had enough self-awareness to say, "I'm feeling angry." As our counselor talked about her observations, I realized that the reason I felt overwhelmed was my inability to admit that I had been in the wrong. To admit fault was just too painful: it was shameful to acknowledge I had failed in being the kind of husband I wanted to be. That sense of shame was driving me to shift blame somewhere else.

As we drove home after that meeting, I took some time to think and pray about what had happened. Because of all those years of pastors warning me about shame, I was equipped to respond to it. If I could find the courage to acknowledge my fault, I knew that God would forgive me, and Katie would too. Then it would be possible to keep talking about how to strengthen our relationship without the need to blame. Until then, though, I hadn't been equipped to recognize shame. In that instance, it was hiding behind my anger. It sometimes hides in other guises, too.

Even though I've known about shame for years, I'm just starting to get to know how my own shame feels. I'm noticing the emotional aspects of how I experience sin and repentance. As I do, I see that shame has been lurking within the nooks and crannies all the while. In the past, my "get things done" approach led me to focus on what to do when I realized I'd sinned. I would try to identify the sin specifically, and then pray to God, confessing it. I would also often confess it to someone else, a truly helpful practice I learned at my church as a teenager. After that, I would try to forget about it and move on. If I still had lingering negative feelings (which I often did), I would ask God to strengthen me and help me to receive his grace.

Now, instead of just focusing on what to do, I'm also noticing what I feel. When I realize I've sinned, I'm initially overwhelmed by a sense of wrongness about who I am. I don't measure up. I didn't do it right. It feels like the world is falling apart, and I scramble for control. Importantly, I've also noticed this exact same feeling when I fail in any way, even in ways that can't really be called sin, such as making a grammar error in an email at work, or forgetting an item on my to-do list. It's the feeling I got when Miss Bertsche marked my handwriting as Satisfactory instead of Excellent: this is wrong; it must be fixed, or else I will amount to nothing. Although I've been feeling that feeling for years, I've rarely recognized it as unhealthy self-condemnation. Instead, I've figured it's just a correct, rational response to doing something wrong or making a mistake. It's what's so often motivated me to do well, to be a good Christian. Unbeknownst to me, I've been running my "get things done" machine on a self-condemnation engine.

One reason it was hard for me to identify the feeling of shame is what I imagined when pastors talked about it. I always assumed someone who had a problem with shame must struggle with negative self-talk, consciously questioning their worth or worthiness of love. Many people do struggle with shame in that form. But I tended to indulge in a paradoxically critical and positive kind of self-talk: "This is unacceptable. I'm so smart. I do things right. I have to fix this, to keep things that way." It was my self-confident perfectionism which both fed on and hid the shame. Combined with my sureness that I had the theological basics down, it led me to spiritualize my desperate need for control. Sometimes even confession to God or to another person was just part of my attempt to restore order and my own self-image. Similarly, in moments of conflict with Katie when I blamed her, I could rationalize my controlling attitude as a form of "healthy confrontation."

As I continue to attend to my emotions, I believe I'm learning to distinguish between toxic, self-condemning shame and genuine contrition. Contrition still feels "bad"; it's a form of grief or sorrow. Yet it doesn't feel like the world will cease to exist if I acknowledge my failures. When I feel overwhelmed, I can pause before launching into blame or frantic "fix-it" behavior. Instead, I can take a deep breath, remember that God is still holding onto me in love even as I realize how I've failed, and then move into genuine confession.

Learning how shame feels has been a powerful turning point in learning how to be a bad Christian. Refusing to recognize shame is one thing that's kept me in the posture of the Pharisee, focusing on how well I'm doing, because admitting I haven't done well is unacceptable. So when I recognize the voice of shame, I can rebuke it with the truth of the Gospel. It's safe to admit I've sinned, because God's mercy is available. It's safe to make a mistake; the world will not come to an end if the budget spreadsheet isn't perfect. God will still provide for me, and for Katie.

Here is where I can come back to the teaching of Jesus. The old rule said that murderers are liable to judgment; Jesus says that anger makes me liable to judgment. But he's not giving me a new law to follow that says, "Don't be angry." Jesus does not offer law, but new life: "For the law was given through Moses; grace and truth came through Jesus Christ" (John 1:17 ESV). Dallas Willard, one of the best interpreters of Jesus' teaching about anger, says this:

> *Jesus is giving us a revelation of the preciousness of human beings. He means to reveal the value of persons. Obviously merely not killing others cannot begin to do justice to that* . . . . *[Jesus] is taking us deeper into the kind of beings we are, the kind of love God has for us, and the kind of love that, as we share it, brings us into harmony with his life. No one can be*

> *"right" in the kingdom sense who is not transformed at this level. And then, of course, the issue of not being wrongly angry, not expressing contempt . . . and so on is automatically taken care of.*

Jesus' teaching is that the kind of heart that reacts to others in anger is a heart that will lead me toward God's judgment. Anger is a sin that fails to honor the precious people whom God has created. When I routinely directed anger at Katie over money matters, I was failing to see her as the kind of being to whom such anger simply should not be directed. She is too precious for that. The solution, though, is not to try and double-down on controlling behavior ("Don't be angry!"). That approach never brings real, lasting change. The solution is to allow God to work on the heart, to make space for him to address what leads to the anger in the first place. Once that area is touched by his healing hand, the teaching about anger becomes possible—even easy—to follow.

Responding to Fear and Anxiety

Fear is another negative emotion I had hoped counseling would "fix." After all, the Bible tells us that prophets, angels, and Jesus himself repeatedly said, "Don't be afraid." Isn't that another rule to follow? Isn't "not being afraid" something that mature Christians should be able to do?

Yet with fear, as with sadness and anger, the way forward looks different than I expected. Like other emotions, fear can come upon us unexpectedly and unbidden. You can't stop being afraid just by direct effort of willpower. It's easier to ignore fear than to confront it. Even when ignored, though, fear can drive our behavior in ways we may not recognize. Pretending we're not afraid does not solve the problem of fear's power in our lives. Like with anger, what we need is change in the heart, not a rule to follow. We see this in Jesus' words on fear and anxiety:

> "Therefore I tell you, do not worry about your life, what you will eat or drink; or about your body, what you will wear. Is not life more than food, and the body more than clothes? Look at the birds of the air; they do not sow or reap or store away in barns, and yet your heavenly Father feeds them. Are you not much more valuable than they? Therefore do not worry about tomorrow, for tomorrow will worry about itself. Each day has enough trouble of its own." MATTHEW 6:25-26, 34 NIV

I always like to imagine Jesus saying "tomorrow will worry about itself" with a laugh. Days don't have feelings! It's as if Jesus knows how hard it is for us to let go of anxiety and fear, so he suggests tomorrow is taking on the responsibility of worrying. Don't worry about worrying; tomorrow's got it handled. So often in my life, I have just the opposite attitude. Tomorrow is not going to worry about itself, I say. If anyone's going to worry about it, it has to be me. And I do. And I plan. It's the responsible thing to do. But "being responsible" can also be a convenient cover for being afraid. This became clear to me shortly after Katie became a nurse.

After obtaining her nursing license one February, Katie began a job at a local rehabilitation hospital. She still needed to complete her bachelor's degree, so we planned for her to attend a night class program that fall. About six weeks into the program, Katie was exhausted. Struggling to stay afloat, she began to relapse into her eating disorder. Neither of us wanted her to quit school, but we felt like we were at the end of our rope. Katie was doing worse, not better, despite support from friends and family and good doctors. We met with a pastor at our church who listened to us describe our situation and encouraged us to make a change. "You need to take this seriously," she said. "Taking care of Katie is what you should be giving your focus and creative energy to, even if it means giving up on your timeline."

After this conversation, we decided it would be best for Katie to drop out of school for the time being. Making that decision felt totally unnatural to me. Fears about the future crowded in. If Katie didn't finish her degree this year, when would she? What if she never did? Less education can mean less mobility; would we miss out on opportunities because of this delay? Then, not long after stopping school, Katie suggested she also take a leave of absence from work to confront the gravity of her mental health needs. This time, I put up a fight. Quitting school should be enough, I said. We needed some sort of stability in our lives! We needed some sort of plan.

Still, Katie held her ground. She knew she needed the time off, so that she could participate in a local eating rehab program. Eventually, she won me over. I realized sticking to the plan would be getting in the way of what Katie needed. It wasn't "responsible" to object to a leave of absence; it was just fearful. She took six weeks off. That time ended up creating room for her to not only rebuild a healthy relationship with food, but to begin finding healing for deeper wounds as well. The anxiety I had about her time off melted away as I saw what a difference in her life it was making. To my surprise, departing from the plan and doing the "irresponsible" thing of taking a break from school proved to bear much fruit in Katie's life, and in our marriage.

With anger, it took me some time to realize I've been running my "get things done" machine on a self-condemnation engine. In much the same way, it only slowly dawned on me that I've been running my "follow the plan" machine on a fear engine. I plan in order to make sure that good things will happen to me and bad things won't. When I don't have a plan, I feel naked and vulnerable. Anything could happen! Katie quitting school and taking a leave of absence from work exposed those fears. It showed how attached I was to my plan, my sense of structure, my illusion of control over the future. But when I found the courage to depart from the plan, things turned out for the best. Tomorrow worried about itself.

For me, then, fear was not something I had to "fix"; it was something I had to acknowledge. When I didn't pay attention to my fear, it was easy to rationalize my commitment to the plan as the "responsible" thing to do. But when I did realize the fears that were at play, the right course of action also became clear. I was able to respond to my own fears, and to Katie's real needs, at the heart level. The truth of the Gospel is that God takes care of the birds, and they aren't very good at planning. He'll also take care of us when our circumstances carry us beyond what we can plan for. Making the decision to let go of the plan, and of six weeks' income, required me to trust in God's goodness. And once I made that decision, God's provision for us strengthened both my faith and my courage.

Experiencing Joy

Sadness, anger, shame, fear, anxiety: getting to know these negative emotions has been a surprisingly positive adventure. God can be present with me in sadness, his grace can address the source of my anger and shame, and his provision can make a way forward even when I'm afraid. In the moment, these intertwined feelings still can overwhelm me. They're complicated. They take energy. But I have hope that God is also at work it the middle of it all.

The most important lesson I've learned about negative emotions is that, right alongside them, it's possible to experience what the Bible calls joy. Jesus is our great model in this regard. The writer of the letter to the Hebrews describes joy as Jesus' motivation in his sacrifice: "Jesus . . . for the joy that was set before him endured the cross, despising the shame" (12:2 ESV). At the same time, we have clear accounts that Jesus felt anxiety and sorrow leading up to his passion. In the garden of Gethsemane, contemplating his impending suffering, he tells his disciples, "My soul is overwhelmed with sorrow to the point of death" (Matthew 26:38 ESV). He is also described as being "greatly distressed and troubled" and "in agony" at this juncture (Mark 14:33; Luke 22:44 ESV). The prophecies we find in Isaiah, looking ahead to the trials of the coming Messiah, bestow on him the epithet "Man of Sorrows" (53:3). The joy that was motivating Jesus did not consist in the absence of negative emotions or serious pain.

Certain Christian thinkers try to get at this idea by saying that "joy is different than happiness." We can experience joy even when we're sad and suffering. At the same time, this kind of distinction between joy and happiness can be a bit misleading. Sometimes people will speak as though joy is somehow beyond our emotions: it's the knowledge of God's goodness even if we feel terrible. But this kind of attitude actually makes joy inaccessible and abstract. Joy must be something we can feel! And it must have something in common with happiness.

Matthew writes about the Magi looking for the one to be born King of the Jews. They arrive at Bethlehem: "And behold, the star that they had seen when it rose went before them until it came to rest over the place where the child was. When they saw the star, they rejoiced exceedingly with great joy" (2:9-10 ESV). Another translation says "they were overwhelmed with joy" (NRSV). And one paraphrase puts it: "Their joy knew no bounds!" (TLB). This passage does not invite us to imagine the Magi stoically gaining deeper mental certitude about God; it leads us to imagine them breathless, rushing toward the star. They forget the ache of many months of travel as they drive the caravan forward. They are about to meet the king!

Or, consider Paul's words to the Thessalonians: "For this reason, brothers and sisters, during all our distress and persecution we have been encouraged about you through your faith. For we now live, if you continue to stand firm in the Lord. How can we thank God enough for you in return for all the joy that we feel before our God because of you? Night and day we pray most earnestly that we may see you face to face and restore whatever is lacking in your faith" (1 Thessalonians 3:7-10 NRSV). Paul and his companions do not just know about the Thessalonians' faith; it causes them to feel great joy, which overflows in gratitude to God.

But also note that Paul feels this joy in the middle of distress and persecution. Joy is not the simple happiness of painlessness. It is rather the deep happiness of confidence in God's goodness and provision, which can be felt even in the midst of pain, right alongside the negative emotions that naturally arise from difficult circumstances. In their book *The Cry of the Soul*, Christian psychologist Dan Allender and theologian Tremper Longman III describe the joy we find in God: "It is a joy in the midst of suffering because we know that the core of this goodness can never be removed from us—that core is God Himself. This joy is not a superficial response that ignores the problems in our lives, but a profound emotion that is confident in facing the darkness with open eyes. It is a joy that issues in thanksgiving and praise: a joy that leads to worship."

Our joy is naturally confirmed and increased when we give thanks for particular instances of God's provision. The Thessalonians standing firm in their faith gave Paul deeper joy. Elsewhere he writes to them, "For what is our hope or joy or crown of boasting before our Lord Jesus at his coming? Is it not you? Yes, you are our glory and joy!" (1 Thessalonians 2:19-20 NRSV). As a good spiritual father, Paul is deeply moved with desire for his children in the Lord to be faithful to Jesus right up until he comes. Seeing that they are walking in the way of Jesus broadens his experience of joy. But causes of joy do not have to be so spiritual. Whatever we present to God with a grateful heart can deepen our joy in him, whether it's the shape of a cloud, the texture of a raspberry, or the touch of a loved one.

For me, the joy of simple gratitude for such unplanned gifts has also served as a cure for the shame-based law of getting things done and the fear-based law of following the plan. Not long ago, I went for a walk in the evening. The night was comfortably cool, with a misty rain falling so gently it was only visible in the circle of light just at the top of each streetlamp. I picked up a red maple leaf off of the sidewalk. It had an elegance in its fragility, with a latent story of life etched in its veins, even now that it was fallen from the tree. It had a certain homey, comforting quality I have always found in Midwestern autumns: a gift of vibrant color in the most ordinary thing. I decided to take the leaf home. It's sitting on my nightstand now as I write. In moments like this, God is teaching me the dignity and worth of things which do not accomplish anything, but are simply his gifts to me.

I may not be the only Christian in need of such a cure. I remember once reading a book written by an influential pastor. He tells the story of a retired couple who each day of their retirement go to the beach and collect seashells. Eventually, they die and have to give an account of their lives before God, and all they have to show for their final years is their collection of seashells. The pastor writes: "Picture them before Christ at the great day of judgment: 'Look, Lord. See my shells.' That is a tragedy."

The story is meant to illustrate that we shouldn't fritter away our lives in frivolous pursuits, but rather keep going at full tilt in doing good works right up until our dying day. Don't waste your life on seashells! I think in that story there's a valid critique of the vision of slovenly, self-centered retirement and life in general that is part of our cultural narrative. But it doesn't seem to make room for experiences like my walk in the rain, nor for gifts from God like the red maple leaf. That leaf does not get anything done for the kingdom of God. It does not help me follow any plan. Even so, it is a gift from God to me. It expands my joy.

The story of the seashells is one-sided. It focuses on what we are or aren't doing for God. But I think on Judgment Day what will matter most is the kind of people we have become. Paul writes to the Philippians of his prayers, "that you may . . . be pure and blameless for the day of Christ, filled with the fruit of righteousness that comes through Jesus Christ, to the glory and praise of God" (1:10-11 ESV). That fruit of righteousness is not a catalogue of good deeds, but rather the quality of our interior life, an interior life that includes the virtue of joy: "For the kingdom of God is. . . righteousness and peace and joy in the Holy Spirit" (Romans 14:17 NRSV). The question to ask now, in light of the coming judgment, is not "What am I getting done?" but rather, "Am I on my way to being suffused with the joy of God in my attitudes and aspirations?"

I was sharing these thoughts with one of my pastors, and she recommended I do just what the author-pastor suggests. Picture the couple on the day of judgment saying, "Look, Lord. See our shells." But now imagine that they have gathered these shells in gratitude, as part of a life lived in joyful love of God and others. What do you think Jesus will say in response? It turns out not to be a tragedy at all. He will take great delight in them, and in the gifts they have received! If it's the kind of person I'm becoming that ultimately matters, not just what I get done or how well I plan, then any time

I pass experiencing God's love for me is time well invested. Even the time it takes to notice the gift of a leaf, or a seashell.

Hard-wrought Joy

As much as giving thanks to God for his good gifts can increase our joy, there's an even deeper experience that can come in the darkness of suffering. Earlier, we saw that Allender and Longman connect joy to suffering: "It is a joy in the midst of suffering because we know that the core of this goodness can never be removed from us—that core is God Himself." But how can we find out that God's goodness is all we need? We have to know what it's like to lose some of the other good things we lean on. To learn that God's goodness can never be removed from us, even in suffering and loss, we have to experience suffering and loss. This idea runs against our natural inclinations. Wouldn't it make more sense for God to just make life better and better for his children? Doesn't any good parent want to protect their children from suffering?

Katie and I have a two-year-old goddaughter named Caitlyn. A year ago, when she was learning to walk, we witnessed her surmount obstacles of all kinds. As she pulled herself up on the furniture around the house, and began to find her own wobbly sense of balance, she exposed herself to all sorts of new risks. She could fall down. She could bump into things. But her parents didn't prevent her from exploring, because they knew that life on the other side of standing is better. When Caitlyn was younger, we each had to hold her all the time. Now, we can take away our hand and see her standing fast on her own two feet.

When we're in a season of consolation, grateful to God for the signs of his love in everyday things, he is holding us and supporting us. When we enter into a season of desolation, and the world turns to ash around us, he is letting us learn to stand. I have to admit I didn't come up with this analogy; I stole it from C.S. Lewis, and he puts it so well himself: "Sooner or later [God] withdraws, if not in fact, at least from their conscious experience, all those supports and incentives. He leaves the creature to stand up on its own legs—to carry out from the will alone duties which have lost all relish. It is during such trough periods, much more than during the peak periods, that it is growing into the sort of creature He wants it to be."

We all admire people whose generosity and joy continues unabated even in the bleakest of circumstances. Suffering is the training ground in which such people are formed. When you know the joy of God's goodness even when walking through the valley of the shadow of death, it solidifies into a deeper, stronger thing than before. It becomes a hard-wrought joy, one that no one can ever take away from you.

The difficulties I have faced do not even begin to compare with those of so many others: the truly poor, the desperately ill, those who face degradation and persecution for their faith. So far, bereavement has played only a minor role in my life. But I have heard stories of people in the worst situations rising up into their best selves by the grace of God. And I've had the privilege of seeing this dynamic in the lives of a few people whom I personally know.

When I was a child, the children's pastor of my home church was a woman named Margie. She is still active in parish life today and was recently ordained. Margie has a profound gift of spiritual motherhood. When you are in her presence, you immediately feel known and loved. Just today, I was speaking with one of our youth ministry leaders, who said the young men in his small group were crying as they shared vulnerably with one another last night following a talk Margie had given on the love of God. This kind of penetrating, heart-level ministry of teaching and pastoring is simply the norm with Margie. She also brings an infectious enthusiasm and disarming sense of humor into all of her work.

When I was in elementary school, Margie married John, our worship pastor. We were a small church at the time, and Margie invited all of the elementary school children to sing at her wedding. I remember watching Margie cry through the entire service. John had made the unusual choice of leading worship at his own wedding, but at the time it seemed perfectly natural to me. John was always the one leading worship at our church services! And when John led worship, it was like the whole room was lifted into the presence of God at once. He was an unusual man in many ways, possessed of a rare intellect and refined tastes in both opera and dining. His idiosyncrasies were matched only by the depth of his love for the Lord and for people in pain.

Over the next few years, John and Margie had two children named Charlotte and Josiah. Not long after Josiah's birth, John was diagnosed with cancer. With treatment, he went into remission. Then, he was diagnosed again, with a more aggressive kind. His normal ebullience slowly withered into frailty and quiet. He had to stop working, and struggled daily with intense pain. Here's a description of some of his symptoms that he wrote at the time: "my bones continue to be shaky, shriveled, eaten up and made progressively convoluted. For example, my right rib cage has several tumors growing there, whether breaking down the bone, penetrating it, or using it as a basis to penetrate the lungs. I've noticed in the last few days that it takes more fast, short breathing even to walk slowly, or to speak full sentences or to vocalize loudly." It became clear John would not survive. Charlotte was five, and Josiah was two.

In this suffering, John still ministered the love of God to other people. Here are some selections from his blog during the final months of his illness: "As for one of the more positive things that seems to come within our privilege, I've gotten to pray for several people at their periods of deepest pain where they are heading into hospice care[.]" "I think I already mentioned how much I've come to love the way that my father and I can pray Morning Prayer and then Compline together. It is time more fulfilling than I've yet had with him in my life. . . . And I can't stop without mentioning my mother: great conversations, daily shots and medications, freshly squeezed vegetable and fruit juices . . . [I am] incredibly blessed. I can barely imagine the riches at the end of each day."

Margie also found strength in sharing her experience through a blog: "I have walked a journey of bare-bones humanity. I get up, I do what is before me. I listen for the Lord. My only gift is to simply say, 'Yes Lord.' My gift is to obey and trust. That is all that is possible. I see no other road."

When John did pass away, our whole community grieved. In addition to her own bereavement as a wife, Margie was left with the challenge of being a single mom. In the years since, her children have grown up without their father. Yet Margie has borne out the life of God in this profound loss. She has raised her children with affection and wisdom. She has built up our church community. Countless people have drawn close to God in the midst of their own suffering through her ministry of listening and prayer. Her laughter is as infectious as ever.

Margie speaks sometimes on the subject of "redemptive suffering." "Redemption" is an economic term: Katie and I recently redeemed some savings bonds. They were intrinsically almost worthless, just scraps of paper. But when they were redeemed, they turned out to be incredibly valuable. In our lives, suffering can be like that. It seems pointless. What good can come of it? But God can miraculously transform it into his life. He can redeem it for joy.

Margie and John's lives have shown me that hard-wrought joy

is real, not just an idea. In my own life, I'm just starting to take steps toward this kind of joy as I experience suffering. But when I do—when Katie is in pain, or her various health needs go beyond available treatment, when I feel the weight of trying to provide for her—I want to trust that God is letting me learn how to stand. I want to believe that if I hang on, I'll experience God's goodness in ways I haven't before.

James writes, "My brothers and sisters, whenever you face trials of any kind, consider it nothing but joy, because you know that the testing of your faith produces endurance; and let endurance have its full effect, so that you may be mature and complete, lacking in nothing" (1:2-4 NRSV). There are aspects of our life in God that we can only access through suffering. Facing trials allows us to grow up, so that we are lacking in nothing. Christian therapist Andrew Bauman writes, "If you never allow yourself to feel the pain of loss, the betrayal of hope, you will certainly not feel the depth of true joy. Grief serves as a shovel for the soul. It digs, mines, and excavates painfully, at times violently. Grief digs to make space for deep delight to enter those vacant spaces. This is the posture of vulnerability; it is both terrifying and stirring, and a prerequisite for a broken heart and full life."

This pattern of finding joy "works" because we do not have to make it work; the Holy Spirit works it within us: "we rejoice in our sufferings, knowing that suffering produces endurance, and endurance produces character, and character produces hope, and hope does not put us to shame, because God's love has been poured into our hearts through the Holy Spirit who has been given to us" (Romans 5:3-5 ESV). It is not our power, but the power of God's Spirit, which brings life out of suffering.

And God does not ask of us anything he has not already done himself. Jesus told his disciples, "As the Father has loved me, so have

I loved you. Abide in my love. If you keep my commandments, you will abide in my love, just as I have kept my Father's commandments and abide in his love. These things I have spoken to you, that my joy may be in you, and that your joy may be full" (John 15:9-11 ESV). It is the joy of Jesus himself that we enter into as we abide in his love. This is the work of the Spirit. It is not a joy that we manufacture; it is a joy that we receive. And, just like Jesus, we enter into it through laying everything down at God's feet. We die with Christ, and we share in his resurrection life.

Feeling with God

For me, dying with Christ and sharing his life has required me to pay much more careful attention to my emotions than I have in the past. When I don't pay attention to my emotions, I can have all the right theological ideas, but I just don't see how they actually apply to my situation. We have a vocabulary for failing to understand something: a particularly hard idea might go "over my head." I've had a different problem: it's not the abstract idea that's hard to grasp; it's the concrete manifestation of that idea in my own emotions that goes "over my heart." What I've needed is not a new idea, but a new self-awareness so that the old idea can "take" in my life.

If we're blind to our own emotions, as I have often been, the very enemies that good Christian teaching warns us against can still sneak into our practice of life with God, wrecking havoc all the more effectively because they remain invisible. If, by God's grace, we come to see our emotions more clearly, then his truth can work its way through our whole personality, bringing his new life. He can redeem the pain we feel. We can enter into the joy of Jesus. No matter what we feel, we can feel it in God's presence, and he will bless it and give it back to us as something beautiful and good.

CHAPTER 4

GIVING AND RECEIVING ATTENTION

My brother and I used to play a game when he was about eight years old and I was about four: Dad would be getting ready to leave for work in the morning, on the verge of stepping outside, and we would each grab one of his legs and wrap ourselves around it, weighing him down to keep him from going out the door. My mother has a photograph of this morning drama unfolding: my face is bright with the laughter of un-self-conscious affection, while my brother wears a mischievous smirk. Dad is laughing, too. He wasn't bothered by the demand that he give us a few seconds more of his attention before, finally, leaving for his work day.

Moments like that give us a picture of the human heart. We can't help but look for someone to look at us, to attend to us. We are fashioned to receive loving attention, and we thrive when we get it. Our need for attention is so profound it reveals itself at the earliest ages in how our body develops. Children who suffer neglect are more prone to sickness and less physically resilient. Receiving the affectionate, unhurried gaze of a parent builds a foundation for emotional and physical thriving.

Even the most dedicated parents cannot provide perfect attention to their children. Our hunger goes too deep for even those closest to us to satisfy it, limited human beings that they are. I'm not a psychologist, but I imagine that each of us, as we get older, begins to develop a gap, a kind of "attention debt" that grows every time our valid need for attention goes unmet in some small way. The longing gradually shifts to an ache, which can throb in the background of our lives for years, perhaps for many of us so quietly we don't notice it or have words for it.

As that ache drives us, we seek ways to alleviate it. So we tune in to the people around us and determine who's willing to pay attention to us, and what we have to do to get it. Our language about attention speaks to this way of thinking about it as a transaction. We speak of paying attention more often than giving attention. We need as many payments as we can get to patch over that continually growing debt.

We learn to look for payments early. In second grade, I was mystified by my classmate Connor, who always seemed to be getting into trouble. He was already a skillful class clown, knowing just the right way to make a silly comment or act out to make everyone laugh. Of course, sometimes the best laugh comes at the expense of the lesson, and Connor was certainly willing to break the rules or disregard teachers' instructions if it played well. This kind of behavior made no sense to me at the time: I was already a dutiful student, and eager to follow all the rules and then some. I knew that teachers praised students like me, who always did what was expected of them. Why didn't Connor get it?

In hindsight, it's clear to me that Connor and I were more alike than either of us could realize at the time. He had discovered that humor, and a bit of mischief, brought him the attention of his classmates. I had discovered that obedience and diligence brought me the attention of my teachers. We each fought hard for the attention we had the skill to obtain.

Fighting for attention can wear us out. For me, at least, the pattern of dutiful achievement already in place by second grade has been a hard road to follow into adulthood. In school, every little piece of effort for a class would receive some sort of attention. The quizzes would get graded, the papers read, the comments in class listened to. Teachers have to pay attention to their students' work; it's their job. But in the jobs I've held as an adult, much of what I do has often gone unnoticed. When I worked in an administrative role at my local church, I knew that organizing the details of worship services was intrinsically valuable, but often if what I was working on was really going well, then people wouldn't comment on it, or even think about it. I can't shrink the attention debt just by "doing my work" like I used to. If I want attention, I feel like I have to fight for it.

This attention debt can wear people out in a different way, too. Some people aren't trying hard to get others' attention, but instead have given up on hoping they'll ever get it. This unresolved hurt of isolation can lead to all kinds of coping patterns: losing oneself in work for its own sake, substance abuse and other addictions, or simply profound loneliness. A silent longing for genuine connection haunts our cities and the many communities where true communion remains elusive.

However you've looked for attention in your life, I bet that you've felt worn out by the gap between the attention you need and the attention you get. No matter what we do, we come up short.

We need a different source of attention than what we can get others to pay us through our own efforts. We need loving attention which we can always count on, a kind of attention that's as steady and as deep as the need we feel. We need God's attention.

God's Attention to Us

The Bible provides a dynamic vision of God's attention to his children. In the book of 2 Chronicles, we find the words of the little-known prophet Hanani that "the eyes of the LORD range throughout the entire earth, to strengthen those whose heart is true to him" (2 Chronicles 16:9 NRSV). I love that image of God's eyes. He is not passively waiting for people to impress him; he is actively looking for those who need his strength. The same idea appears in Psalm 33:

> *Truly the eye of the LORD is on those who fear him,*
>   *on those who hope in his steadfast love,*
> *to deliver their soul from death,*
>   *and to keep them alive in famine.* PSALM 33:18-19 NRSV

Here we see the eye of God resting on us even in the middle of our distress. Our soul may be in danger of death, but God sees and delivers us. We may find ourselves in a time of famine, but God feeds us. He is paying attention.

In the New Testament, Jesus expresses this same posture of seeing and seeking people. In John's account of Andrew bringing his brother Simon to Jesus, he writes, "Jesus looked at him and said, 'You are Simon son of John. You will be called Cephas' (which, when translated, is Peter)" (John 1:42 NIV). I love that the text says that Jesus looked at Simon Peter. He paid attention to him, and then he said words that would change his life. In the story about Jesus' encounter with the rich young ruler, Mark writes that "Jesus looked at him and loved him." (Mark 10:21 NIV). Luke tells us that when he was teaching the people and confronting the teachers of the law, "Jesus looked directly at them" (Luke 20:17 NIV). Jesus does not have an efficiency bias. He moves slowly enough to really look at people.

We also see Jesus' attentiveness in his first interactions with a man named Nathanael:

Philip found Nathanael and said to him, "We have found him about whom Moses in the law and also the prophets wrote, Jesus son of Joseph from Nazareth." Nathanael said to him, "Can anything good come out of Nazareth?" Philip said to him, "Come and see." When Jesus saw Nathanael coming toward him, he said of him, "Here is truly an Israelite in whom there is no deceit!" Nathanael asked him, "Where did you get to know me?" Jesus answered, "I saw you under the fig tree before Philip called you." Nathanael replied, "Rabbi, you are the Son of God! You are the King of Israel!" (John 1:45-49 NRSV)

Even before Nathanael found out about Jesus, Jesus had gotten to know him. He saw him under the fig tree. He knew his character. What's more, when Nathanael realized that Jesus knew him for who he really was, Nathanael suddenly saw Jesus for who he really was. Receiving Jesus' attention to him somehow opened up his eyes and made it possible for him to truly pay attention to Jesus.

Reading a passage like this, we can extend the narrative to our own lives. Wherever we are sitting, Jesus is paying attention to us there, even before we are paying any attention to him. He knows just how we are and what makes us uniquely us. Not only that, but like he did for Peter and for Nathanael, he wants to speak to us and tell us what is most true about ourselves.

Sometimes we need a concrete experience of this dynamic in order for it to come home for us. It's one thing to cognitively understand that God knows us and wants to speak into our lives; it's another to actually hear his voice, to feel his loving gaze. For me, one of the most powerful moments of feeling God's attention like that came during my confirmation when I was in seventh grade. Confirmation, a kind of liturgical coming-of-age ceremony practiced in certain Christian traditions, was a big deal at our church. It meant taking a ten-week class about the Christian faith and life, making a public declaration of commitment to Jesus, and then getting prayed for by the bishop in a special church service. The morning of that service, I was all excitement. Every detail filled the air with a sense of celebration, from the verses my youth pastor picked out and read for each student, to the red of the bishop's robe, to the applause of the congregation at the end. But there's one moment that I'll never forget. After the service, one of our pastors named Karen pulled me aside. She said, "When the bishop was praying for you, I received a word from the Lord for you, that you will be his teacher." A teacher who belongs to the Lord—what a word! At such a young age, I admit it may have even gone to my head. But any gift of teaching I had at that time was undeveloped. It would only gradually emerge in the coming years how much I truly came alive when I had the chance to teach others, and specifically to teach them about Jesus. I leaned into those experiences with all the more confidence because of the word that Pastor Karen had shared with me. As I stepped into teaching, I felt that I was following a way that God had prepared for me. He saw me, and knew me, and told me who I was before I could know for myself.

Perhaps you can name similar moments, when God has looked

on you with love, and you've known it. Or maybe you've never had an encounter like that, and you wonder if it's possible. Regardless, it is so easy to forget about God's attention. Despite experiences like my confirmation, when God's attention feels so clear, I still find myself scrambling to pay off my attention debt. I look for others' validation, counting how many cards I get on my birthday and how many likes I get on my Facebook posts. I habitually look for attention in many places. Some of this is good, and unavoidable: I need to receive attention from other human beings to live an emotionally healthy life. But I wonder if my habits are synced up to the truths of Scripture. What can I do to live as though God is eager to pay attention to me?

Our Attention to God

When someone enjoys paying attention to us, it makes it so easy for us to pay attention to them. I think of my friend Nephtali. Whenever I bump into him, he always has time to talk with me for a few minutes, even in the middle of a busy day. With Neph, it's never just chit-chat, either, but a true and heartfelt conversation. He offers the rare gift of steady attention in the middle of a distracted world. It's no surprise, then, that I gravitate toward Neph in social gatherings. I make time to hang out with him. Receiving such genuine attention makes me pay attention to him.

In my walk with God, too, remembering the Bible's teaching that he is already paying attention to me can lead me to pay attention to him. God's attention is always available, but it's easy to miss it. In order to receive that loving, affectionate embrace, I have to turn toward it with open arms. I have to pay attention to God paying attention to me. Dallas Willard put it, "You see, God doesn't wish to overwhelm us. He's put us in a position where our will can go in either direction. We are responsible for our decision. It's what we choose to see that matters. In order for us to have that choice, God leaves things so that we have to seek them." God will not force himself on me. The water of his affectionate attention for me runs deeper than I can imagine, but I go thirsty unless I put my bucket down into the well. I've found that doing so involves a few specific tasks. To turn to God's attention, I can ask, open up, wait, and look the cross.

Ask

The Bible not only contains the teaching that God is paying attention to us; it shows us how to put our bucket down into the well of his love. We particularly find this kind of guidance in the Psalms. In these poem prayers, we find that the first step in receiving God's attention is to simply ask for it. Consider these verses from Psalm 17:

> *Hear a just cause, O LORD; attend to my cry;*
> *give ear to my prayer*
>
> *Guard me as the apple of the eye;*
> *hide me in the shadow of your wings*
>
> *As for me, I shall behold your face in righteousness;*
> *when I awake I shall be satisfied, beholding your likeness.*
> PSALM 17:1, 8, 15 NRSV

The psalmist both conveys beautiful images of God's attentive character and asks God to show that character. If I use the words of this prayer, I'm asking God to look after me protectively, treasuring me and guarding me, holding me close like a bird would its chicks. These are images of everyday intimacy, of deep knowing.

The psalmist is confident that he will see God's face and be satisfied. At the same time, this confidence leaves room for asking God to pay attention; these images are offered in the form of requests.

At first blush, it might seem redundant to ask God to do what he is already doing. It's not as though God is distracted, buried in a project, and only looks up at his children when they cry out, "Pay attention to me!" Human parents inevitably disappoint their children's need for attention in this way, but God's love is infinite. He has never been distracted from loving us. He does not need our prayers to remind him to pay attention.

Even so, asking God to pay attention gives voice to our deep longing for his love. The asking is more for us than for God. It puts us in a position in which we are ready to truly receive. Asking does not alter God's basic attitude toward us, nor is it a spiritual hoop that God expects us to jump through before he gives us what we need. Asking accomplishes something substantive and important in us, to prepare us for God's response. If we are unable to ask, there is some genuine problem. Perhaps we are unaware of our need for God's attention, or lack the humility to come to him with our hat in hand and simply request it. If so, asking itself is the best solution. It aligns us to the reality of our need and the abundance of God's grace.

Open Up

Another aspect of receiving God's attention is to open ourselves to him with honesty about the real situation of our lives. Pretending to be happier or more put together than we are closes us off from God. We can only truly meet him when we come to him as we are. Naked emotional honesty with God may not be possible at first, especially if we are just beginning in our walk with him. Like with anyone new, we tend to hedge our confessions, to test the waters. The philosophical knowledge that God already knows our thoughts and feelings doesn't necessarily speed up the process; we have to experientially learn that he is a good Father, willing to really listen to us, by sharing and baring our soul one step at a time.

In the psalms, we see the heartbreaking prayers of men and women who have learned to speak openly with God, without fear. They are asking for God to show up. Consider these passages:

> *Give ear to my prayer, O God;*
> *do not hide yourself from my supplication.*
> *Attend to me, and answer me;*
> *I am troubled in my complaint.*
> *I am distraught* PSALM 55:1-2 NRSV

> *Hear my cry, O God;*
> *listen to my prayer.*
> *From the end of the earth I call to you,*
> *when my heart is faint.* PSALM 61:1-2 NRSV

> *Out of the depths I cry to you, O LORD.*
> *Lord, hear my voice!*
> *Let your ears be attentive*
> *to the voice of my supplications!* PSALM 130:1-2 NRSV

Sometimes the Bible even gives voice to the feeling that God is no longer paying attention:

> *Rouse yourself! Why do you sleep, O Lord?*
> *Awake, do not cast us off forever!*

> *Why do you hide your face?*
> *Why do you forget our affliction and oppression?*
> *For we sink down to the dust;*
> *our bodies cling to the ground.*
> *Rise up, come to our help.*
> *Redeem us for the sake of your steadfast love.*
>
> PSALM 44:23-26 NRSV

If you've journeyed with God for some time, and you feel that longing for his attention, then these passages offer you the space to speak with God frankly about whether you feel like he's paying attention or not. The confidence of faith in God's "steadfast love" is fully compatible with the anxious cry, "Why do you hide your face?" I still find myself hesitant to ask God these kinds of questions. It seems too bold, too self-centered even, to imply that my suffering can justify making such demands of God. It almost seems like I would be accusing God of doing something wrong! When I pray, I tend to qualify any negative statements: "God, I know you're listening, but it just doesn't feel like it." And that kind of timid, qualified cry for help may be a place to start when I feel abandoned. The Scriptures themselves invite us to just call it how it is, to speak from the anguish directly: "Why do you forget our affliction and oppression?" Why aren't you listening to me? Why aren't you paying attention?

While inviting us into honesty about our negative emotions toward God, these passages also evoke a positive expectation of what life with God can be like. The writers call out to God, waiting for him to respond. Behind and beneath their fear and anger, they hold some kind of faith in God's responsiveness. They still believe he is worth talking to. They appeal to his character, his love, as well as his place in their lives: he is still their Lord and God. Their words show that they believe he can do what they are asking of him: give ear, attend, listen, hear. They believe God is the kind of God who pays attention to them, and they're asking why that hasn't been the case lately. You can hear the affection and familiarity in their pleas: "You're not like this, God. You're loving and attentive. What's happened?" These words of abandonment imply the basic attention of God by voicing distress at its absence. The cry of forsakenness is not just found side-by-side with proclamations of faith; in the paradox of prayerful suffering it is itself a cry of faith.

Wait

There is reason to believe that such faith will not be disappointed. Emotional honesty with God may not lead to dramatic epiphanies or sudden breakthroughs. The Bible does not provide any blanket promises of immediate freedom from suffering. Yet many of these passages, even those with the deepest grief, are intertwined with words that attest to the experience of God's goodness and favor. The writers voice their trouble in expectation that God will somehow meet them in the middle of it all. Each of these verses follows one of those above:

> *But I call upon God,*
> *   and the Lord will save me.*
> *Evening and morning and at noon*
> *I utter my complaint and moan,*
> *   and he will hear my voice.*
> *He will redeem me unharmed*
> *   from the battle that I wage,*
> *   for many are arrayed against me.*
>
> PSALM 55:16-18 NRSV

> *Lead me to the rock*
>   *that is higher than I;*
> *for you are my refuge,*
>   *a strong tower against the enemy.*
>
> PSALM 61:2-3 NRSV

These passages call for a practice of waiting on God. Time may pass, with little apparent change in our situation, but even so we remain where we are, and remain open to God. We call on him, trusting that he will save us, that he will redeem us unharmed, that he will be our refuge.

But what does that actually mean? In my experience, prayer does not always lead to an immediate emotional transformation. If I'm in a season of sadness, prayer does not make me immediately happy. If I'm in a season of anxiety, prayer does not make my fears vanish. Even so, there is a deliverance that God gives me when I open myself to him, as I really am. It's not freedom from experiencing negative emotions, but rather freedom from being dominated by them. In God's presence, I find that I can be sad and that being sad won't kill me. I can still feel the tug of anxiety, but I know that Jesus is with me. Even in the middle of pain, I can feel the joy of his love. The difficulty and suffering of life does not have to go away in order for me to receive his attention.

The Apostle Paul described it, "We are afflicted in every way, but not crushed; perplexed, but not driven to despair; persecuted, but not forsaken; struck down, but not destroyed; always carrying in the body the death of Jesus, so that the life of Jesus may also be made visible in our bodies" (2 Corinthians 4:8-10 NRSV). Even when our experience is darkness and death, it can become a place of meeting Jesus, who entered darkness and death for us and speaks his word of new life over the bleakest of circumstances.

Look to the Cross

Paul's words bring us to the heart of receiving God's attention: looking upon the cross of Jesus Christ. The cross is the center of God's attentiveness to us. In another passage, Paul writes, "But God proves his love for us in that while we still were sinners Christ died for us" (Romans 5:8 NRSV). Jesus' sacrifice is the best demonstration of God's basic attitude toward us. He is so for us, so aware of our needs, so willing to do whatever is necessary to help us, that Jesus laid down his life for us. Jesus accomplished that which we could not accomplish for ourselves: he destroyed sin and death by bearing it for us in his own body and rose again to give us eternal life.

On the cross, Jesus also entered into the experience of human suffering. When we are in distress, if we turn our eyes to the cross, we remember we are not alone in whatever pain we face. Jesus has come close to us in suffering itself. When we are in a time of anguish, the cross can be a refuge beyond words and unsatisfactory answers to unanswerable questions. My wife Katie writes of her experience with both physical pain and depression, "Most answers are unhelpful. This is why I keep coming back to Jesus' Passion. Even when nothing gets better, God is with us in Jesus' deepest pain, not even trying to offer encouragements, but just being there. And that is enough."

The seventeenth-century English poet-priest Thomas Traherne wrote of the inexhaustible meaning of the cross: "The Cross is the abyss of wonders, the centre of desires, the school of virtues, the house of wisdom, the throne of love, the theatre of joys, and the place of sorrows; It is the root of happiness, and the gate of Heaven." Traherne's words remind us that the cross is not just the center of God's attention to us. It can also become the center of our attentiveness to God. It is a school, a house of wisdom, which teaches us the goodness of God. When I fix my eyes on Jesus laying down his life, I come closer to God and experience his love more fully. I remember the truths of the Gospel: I am united to Christ's death and resurrection through faith and through baptism. All of me—soul, mind, and body—is incorporated into that supernatural act of God to destroy sin and death forever. This is a spiritual truth, unchanging in the vicissitudes of life, a given and a gift I do not have to earn.

But that central truth is so easy to forget. As frequently as I find myself drawn to other sources of attention, I need reminders of God's deepest attention to me. These reminders can be practical, even mundane: simply seeing or touching a cross can be enough. I find frequent contact with the symbol of the cross to be tremendously helpful. There's one at my desk at work, and another in my bedroom. I wear a cross necklace every day, so that it's always within reach. I'm drawn into reflection on Jesus' sacrifice at church as I look at the large cross at the front of the sanctuary. In whatever form the reminder comes, I need it. God draws me to himself through the cross.

Asking, opening up, waiting, and looking to the cross. As we incorporate these practices into our lives, we begin to experience God's attention to us more fully. That attention slowly fills up the gap in our soul, paying down the attention debt. As we feel more at peace in God's attention, we become less dependent upon frantically extracting attention from others. We loosen our grip on those things which we thought were essential, whether it's the laughter of our classmates and colleagues or the approval of our teachers and bosses. Our knowledge of God's love for us becomes more and more fully part of our lived experience.

Making Time for Attention

This whole process takes time. Giving and receiving attention is not something we can tack on to a long list of other activities. But that hasn't stopped me from trying!

Back when Katie's health was first rapidly deteriorating, while I was distracted with half a dozen ministry responsibilities, Katie initiated what I have come to call our "speed bump" conversation. I was moving so fast I did not really realize how heavy a burden she was carrying as her health needs became increasingly complex. I had my eyes on the path ahead, the things I felt I needed to accomplish. Katie, meanwhile, felt as though I had left her by the side of the road. I wasn't giving her the attention she needed and deserved.

We went for a walk one day in May, and she began to bring up how she felt and what was really going on. Here's a condensed version of our conversation:

Katie: I need you to be home more. I have health issues. I need your support.

Chris: But then I would have to quit some of the things!

Katie: Yes, yes you would.

The conversation pained me because, though I knew that I needed to shift my priorities in order to care for Katie like she needed, I was reticent to let anything go. The law of getting things done felt unbreakable. I argued with Katie, trying to explain how important the things I was doing were to me. After going back and forth for a while, Katie simply said, "I don't know if I have anything more to say, but you need to pray about all of this." She made it clear she thought I was too busy and, if I talked with God, would learn that he thought so too.

Katie was right. When I took some time to pray about everything I was involved in and consider what God was really asking of me, it became painfully obvious that I had submerged myself in ministry activity far beyond what was healthy for our marriage. I was in denial about the amount of everyday attention Katie needed at that juncture of our lives. I didn't want to accept that the difficulties of her illness imposed limits on my life. The truth is, if Katie had not confronted me, I would have simply kept up the same regimen of "work for the kingdom." It was only because she asked me to stop and pay attention that I gave myself permission to listen to God's voice instead of the law of getting things done.

When I did take time to listen for God's voice in prayer, I was surprised by what I discovered. Rather than the unrelenting pressure to perform I usually imposed on myself when I thought about my various projects, I felt a spirit of freedom, and welcome. I did not get the sense that God would be disappointed if I did fewer things, but instead felt as though he was actually excited about what might happen if I had more space in my life. It was as though he was looking forward to spending more time with me. I was intrigued, but still felt nervous about doing less.

A turning point came just a few months later when it was time for me to register for fall classes. One particular concern from the speed bump conversation had been how many seminary classes I would take at one time. I was planning to take two, but Katie thought I should take only one. Initially, I had railed against this suggestion; if I only took one course per term, my degree would take me four or five years to complete! My internal ambition was driving me to get it done faster. At the same time, after talking with Katie and my time in prayer, I was almost certain taking just one class that fall was the right thing to do. So, with trepidation, I only selected one class on the registration form.

When I clicked the final button on the form and stood up from my laptop, I felt a weight I had been carrying within me disappear. I felt peace in the decision. For the first time in a long time, I felt like I could look forward to a term without worrying about how I was going to fit it all in. In the months that followed, I was able to spend more time in prayer and more time with Katie. Our conversations became a main feature of each day rather than an afterthought. God began to meet me in new ways. Making time for attention gave rise to more attention. That initial conversation with Katie led to me asking questions in prayer I wouldn't otherwise have asked. And those questions allowed new patterns of life to emerge, in which hearing God's voice reinforced the freedom I felt from the need to achieve.

I wish I could write that it has simply been one long stretch of continually increasing health in prayer and in our marriage since that fall. But really I've had quite a bit of trouble unlearning the law of getting things done. After a pretty solid semester of room for prayer and conversation with Katie, I began adding additional ministry responsibilities back into my schedule. By March, I was again caught up in the pattern of juggling multiple projects and distracted from Katie's needs. I didn't listen when she again told me she needed more of me than she was getting. I was focused on the future, ignoring the needs of the present, trying to achieve what I felt was necessary. It was in pursuit of the future that I arranged to meet with my pastor friend Trevor and try to convince him to give me a job.

By God's grace, that encounter became another speed bump conversation, in which Trevor challenged me to face the reality of my ministry disorder. It led Katie and I to another round of intentionally cutting back on what I was giving my time to, which in turn again bore fruit as I could give myself more fully to God and to her. (I'll write more about that experience in chapter six.)

I don't imagine that conversation will be the last speed bump I need. But I have realized that I can't fit giving and receiving attention into the margins of my life. I have to make time to receive God's attention to me, and to pay attention to him. When I do, it opens up my heart so I can pay attention to other people as well, especially Katie. Dallas Willard writes, "No time is more profitably spent than that used to heighten the quality of an intimate walk with God. If we think otherwise, we have been badly educated. The real question is, 'Will we take time to do what is necessary for an abundant life and an abundant ministry, or will we try to "get by" without it?'" I am learning that I do not actually "get by" when I don't plan for attention; I simply get better at distracting myself from what's really going on in my soul and in my marriage. I'm a slow learner, but God has not held back from me as I've returned to him, seeking his love and guidance anew. He is always ready to receive me when I remember to come back to him.

Paying Attention to Ourselves

It is this openness of God to us, even in response to our sin and weakness, that also teaches us how to pay the right kind of attention to ourselves. The loving gaze of God allows us to take a hard look at ourselves without fear or shame. We can consider ourselves "with sober judgment," as Paul encouraged his readers, perhaps for the first time (Romans 12:3).

When Winston Churchill turned eighty years old, he was still a politically powerful figure, serving his second term as Prime Minister of the United Kingdom. Yet nearly a decade after his "never surrender" policy had paved the way for the Allied victory over Nazi Germany, Churchill had suffered two strokes and struggled to conceal from his political colleagues and the nation his weakening physical and mental stamina. In honor of his eightieth birthday,

Parliament commissioned artist Graham Sutherland to paint his portrait and presented the painting to Churchill in a televised ceremony. The portrait, unapologetic in its realism, showed the elder citizen seated, worn and aged. Churchill hated it. In a private conversation, he complained, "How do they paint one today? Sitting on a lavatory! Here sits an old man on his stool, pressing and pressing." The painting lingered in the cellar of the Churchill's country estate for some time, until a family secretary arranged for it to be burned.

Perhaps Churchill wished he could have been carved in marble, preserved with youthful vigor and strength as other military heroes have been. Sutherland saw something else in the aging lion. Critics who viewed the painting before it was destroyed wrote of it with admiration, one calling it, "a great artist's vision of a great English warrior." But Churchill himself could not see this greatness in the wrinkles and rolls that Sutherland painted. He could not receive this image of himself in his decline.

Looking at ourselves without illusions is no easy task. We feel the tug of many forces that drive us to develop a false image of ourselves and that distract us from noticing how far that image is from reality. I can sympathize with the good Prime Minister. My personality leads me to value competence, achievement, and correctness, so I find it excruciatingly difficult to admit when I am weak, unimpressive, or wrong. I develop an image of myself as someone who always follows the plan and always gets things done. I often hold onto that image in desperation, afraid that if I let go of it there will be nothing left of me. Or nothing left worth looking at.

Learning to receive God's attention for me is the antidote to that fear. As I realize that he attends to me, regardless of how well or poorly I am doing, regardless of whether I'm impressive or not, I gain the courage to acknowledge my own frailty and limitations—the courage to be a bad Christian.

When I was a child, I loved the book You Are Special written by Max Lucado and illustrated by Sergio Martinez. It tells the story of a town full of wooden people, called Wemmicks, who go around giving each other stars and dots. When a Wemmick is impressed with someone, they give them a star to express their admiration. If they are unimpressed, they give a dot. Punchinello, the story's protagonist, usually only receives dots, but a turning point comes when he meets a Wemmick named Lucia. She has no stars or dots at all; they do not stick to her. Punchinello is shocked, and learns Lucia's secret: she spends time with Eli, the woodcarver. Punchinello goes to meet this maker and begins to learn that he can be free from how others have dotted him, too.

I still love this story, and I understood even as a child that Eli represented God, and that I could learn that I was special by spending time with God, that his voice was more important than other people's voices. I'm so grateful to Lucado and Martinez and the many men and women in my life who helped me learn that lesson early on. But I have to confess that I was always confused and disturbed by one part of the story: I liked that Lucia didn't have to carry around the dots other people had given her. But I couldn't understand why she didn't get to keep her stars! It seemed to me that it would have been better for Eli to get rid of all the bad stuff, but let her hang onto those nice, shiny stickers of approval.

Even now as a grown man, I'm still discovering how deeply I long for approval—from others, from myself, and from God. My story is the mirror image of Punchinello's. It's not that I've usually been given dots in my life, but that I've become skilled at winning stars. And it turns out that stars can be just as much a trap as dots. I trap myself in the anxiety of performance, of doing things just right so that I will be okay, so that I will win the next star.

These habits are so ingrained in me that they are no longer really decisions; they come automatically. We all have deeply-rooted repertoires of behaviors, driven by our need for attention, over which we now have little immediate control. That's why, as Lucado and Martinez so beautifully show, we don't get free from the stickers and dots by trying hard not to let them stick in the moment. We get free by taking time, whenever we can, to spend time with our maker. When we see his face smiling at us, and hear his voice speaking over us with affection, something begins to shift within our souls. The clamoring, desperate longing for stars quiets down, even if only a little at first. And in that growing quiet, space is created in which we can form new patterns of attention to God and others.

CHAPTER 5
ASKING FOR HELP

Katie's health challenges in our second year of marriage pushed me to a place I hadn't been before. Around the same time as our speed bump conversation, but before I had really begun to slow down, I felt caught in the vice of several life stressors at once. I was just beginning seminary classes, facing new challenges at work, and trying to navigate the complexities of Katie's health care. In the midst of her ups and downs, even everyday life felt out of control. I slept longer hours than I usually do and still woke up tired. It became difficult for me to enjoy my work.

As all of this was happening, I focused my attention on the things I needed to accomplish: the homework, the work projects, and whatever practical things Katie needed. Life was tough, but what could I do? Best to plan and get things done, I thought.

Thankfully, others in my life were attentive to my soul when I was not. Pastor Karen (who we met in chapter four at my confirmation) noticed that I wasn't my usual chipper self. She asked me how I was doing in a way that let me know I could really tell her what was going on. As I described the challenges I was facing, Karen listened carefully and exuded warmth and compassion. She asked me if I had a spiritual director, and I said I didn't. She recommended that I get one.

I was tempted to respond, "No, I think I'm okay." I'm not the kind of Christian who needs direction, I thought; I'm pretty good at managing my life with God.

Yet as Karen took my needs seriously, I found that I had permission to take them seriously, too. They surfaced easily when I gave them a chance: I was burned out, anxious, and empty. I was just the sort of person who needed direction. Karen was saying, "You need to ask for help."

Asking for help goes against the grain of our culture. The shape of our educational and economic system rests on an ideal of discrete, self-sufficient individuals rather than, for example, the formation of self-sustaining interdependent communities like the agrarian societies of our ancestors. That's not to say I want to return to an agrarian system, but it's important to acknowledge how the water we swim in may be affecting us. We lionize those whose success is "self-made," as though collaboration and relying on others wasn't a crucial element of every success story. If I say that someone "needs help," I'm not usually paying them a compliment. Asking for help also goes against the grain of my two laws. If I could just get things done and follow the plan, I wouldn't need help. If I were strong and successful in and of myself, I wouldn't need help. If I were a good Christian, I wouldn't need help.

When we ask for help, we reveal our needs to another person.

And revealing our needs always puts us in a position of vulnerability. We can't maintain the illusion that we are somehow invincible or above needs. Brené Brown, a social researcher at the University of Houston, has spoken about this dynamic. Brown tells the story of how she was once trying to discover what allows for meaningful human connection. She conducted interviews and collected data from hundreds of people. She found that some people have "a strong sense of love and belonging"; they experience connection with others in a deep way. Here's where her research about these people led her: "Here's what I found. What they had in common was . . . the courage to be imperfect; they had the compassion to be kind to themselves first and then to others . . . [and] they had connection . . . as a result of authenticity. They were willing to let go of who they thought they should be in order to be who they were." She discovered that the most deeply connected people "fully embraced vulnerability."

The people who experience true connection are those who ask for help. The courage to be imperfect is what we summon when we ask for help. The compassion to be kind to ourselves is what we demonstrate when we ask for help. And what about letting go of who we think we should be, in order to be who we are? This kind of language, coming from a social scientist, might make some Christians feel skittish. Doesn't it sound like moral relativism? But the kind of self-acceptance Brown is describing doesn't have to involve eschewing moral standards. Instead, it means being honest with ourselves and other people about our weakness, our failures, and our sin. It means acknowledging how deeply we need help.

Brown describes how difficult it was to face this reality for herself. Her findings did not come to her as welcome news; only unwillingly did she draw the conclusion that vulnerability matters: "I personally thought it was betrayal. I could not believe I had pledged allegiance to research . . . the definition of research is to control and predict. . . and now . . . my mission to control and predict had turned up the answer that the way to live is with vulnerability, and to stop controlling and predicting." Brown went on to suffer a personal crisis because of this epiphany. In a place of deeply questioning what really matters, she decided to ask for help. She began seeing a therapist, and eventually discovered how to put vulnerability into practice in her own life in a way that transformed her relationships.

Even for the experts, asking for help is hard. But those who find the courage to ask experience life in a new way.

Jesus said, "Ask, and it will be given to you; seek, and you will find; knock, and it will be opened to you. For everyone who asks receives, and the one who seeks finds, and to the one who knocks it will be opened" (Matthew 7:7-8 ESV). I had always assumed that these words were intended as guidance for the life of prayer. God will respond when we ask him for help. So it came to me as a surprise when I read Dallas Willard's interpretation: "the ask-seek-knock teaching first applies to our approach to others, not to prayer to God." Dallas argues that Jesus is teaching us about honoring other people. We do not make demands of them; we ask them for help:

In the very act of asking, in the nature of the request, we acknowledge that the other person can say no . . . Yet we ask, and we are supposed to ask, and in by far the most cases he or she does not say no. "Ask," Jesus said, "and you shall receive. Seek, and you shall find. Knock, and it shall be opened to you." That is how we are to relate to others. And that is the primary intention of this much quoted passage.

This interpretation underscores Jesus' concern that his disciples learn how to ask for help. I'm not supposed to manage my life with God by myself, just asking, and seeking, and knocking in my own prayer. I'm also supposed to go to others in appropriate ways, trusting that they will respond to me with what I need. In this way, prayer and my relationships with other people intertwine with each other. For example, as I ask God to meet me in emotional difficulty, and I open up to trustworthy people in emotional vulnerability, God answers my prayer through them. I feel loved by him in my sadness after sharing it with my counselor or a good friend. I have found Jesus's words to prove true as I have turned to others for help. Almost always, the door opens wide.

Finding Direction

This certainly was the case with seeking out a spiritual director. A few weeks after speaking to Karen, I found myself in the home of a man named George. Clean-cut and trim, sporting a polo and a friendly Walter Cronkite mustache, George still had a certain military bearing ten years out from his retirement as a Navy chaplain, but he wore it lightly. At our first meeting, he radiated discipline and intelligence, and a disarming spirit of welcome and kindness. I immediately felt at home in his study-turned-chapel, which was lined with overfull bookshelves and a dozen volumes scattered elsewhere in the room. Light filtered gently through the windows. George had set up two seats angled slightly towards each other, facing a small table with a candle and a cross. We each sat down, and George began to ask me questions about my life. He was interested in who I was, what I liked to do with my time, my vocational aspirations, my relationship with Katie, and how I prayed. George would occasionally make observations or suggestions, and we ended the hour with a brief time of silence and prayer. We didn't get into anything too profound that first week, but I felt a settledness that often comes only after knowing someone for a good while. I had clearly found someone whom I could trust, and who would listen as I tried to untangle what was going on in my heart and mind, but I suspected I had found even more than that. Over the coming months, George indeed became not only a friend and listener, but also a genuine guide.

It would be misleading to describe what I found in my meetings with George primarily in terms of ideas or principles. Our conversations were often meandering, as I shared my questions and experiences and tried to make sense of my life. Although George was clear that what he offered wasn't counseling, an element of "the talking cure" did feature in our meetings. Talking through things in the presence of an attentive and intelligent listener itself no doubt made a difference. Yet what occurred was more than that. George was not merely attentive, but prayerfully so. It was clear that our talks always took place in the presence of Jesus, and in opening my heart to George's influence I could feel that I was also making myself more available to God's guidance over the matters we discussed. Of course, I knew that I was free at any time to talk with God myself, and that is the main thing George helped me to do better. At the same time, George tangibly ministered the availability of God. Just as Scripture teaches that confessing sin to another person and praying with them can somehow open up the possibility of healing (James 5:16), I found that confessing my various circumstantial and spiritual challenges to George and praying with him opened up new spaces in my soul for God to work.

Despite the benefits of the meetings themselves, George insisted early on that the main thing I should be paying attention to was not what happened when I met with him, but what happened in my own life of prayer during the week. To that end, George helped me begin to make connections between the work of prayer and all of the difficult emotions I was experiencing. Prior to meeting with George, I had developed a habit of praying on Friday, my day off. I would settle into a comfortable chair on the second floor of our local library, looking out the window onto the park below. Away from the rush of the work week, this Friday prayer time became a chance to take a deep breath and reflect on my life without hurry. It was also the one time each week when I was giving myself permission to pay attention to my feelings. I would often begin by journaling about all I had experienced that week, because if I didn't, I wouldn't be able to focus on anything else. After those journaling times, I often did feel better, as though I had somehow given my emotions to the Lord. Still, it felt like I was surfacing to breathe after spending a whole week submerged in the current of anxiety.

I explained this practice to George, expecting him to commend me for my good work in setting aside a regular, extended time for prayer. Instead, he focused on my emotional experience: "When you pray like that, how long after your prayer time does that feeling of peace in the Lord last?" I had to admit the benefit was usually short-lived. I felt at peace and connected to God on Fridays, but harried and distracted the rest of the week. George offered a bit of direction: "How about you set aside shorter times of prayer throughout the week? I think it's more important to have a day-to-day point of connection than to clock a lot of hours all at once." George suggested that these shorter times of prayer might help bring God's peace into the midst of my daily emotional experience. As I changed my habits, I discovered that he was right.

Another practice that George taught me about is the daily Examen. A rather ecumenical Presbyterian, George loaned me a book that described this practice as it is found in the Jesuit tradition and the teachings of St. Ignatius of Loyola. The Examen can take many forms, but it always centers on reviewing one's experiences from the day with an openness to the Lord. In the past, if I ever took time to review my day in prayer, I often did so with a focus on confessing sin: where did I mess up? George said that confession of sin was good and often necessary to the Examen, but also that sin wasn't the only aspect of my experience to consider. I could also pay attention to my feelings, and even learn from them. When did I feel full of life? What was I thankful for? When did I feel drained? What troubled me? As I reflected on these questions with God, not only could I develop a sense of his presence with me in all of my feelings, but I could actually begin to see more of how he was working in my life. The work I did with George in this way anticipated the changes that came later as I began seeing a counselor.

Is it possible I could have learned these lessons without George's help? There's obviously much in my spiritual life that I've received one-on-one with God. Meeting God in prayer and Scripture in times of solitude has been essential to the ongoing process of change in my life. But I can't imagine I would have entered into that change as fully without George. On my own, I wouldn't have entered into the new, healthier patterns of prayer and sharing my emotions with God that enriched my life so much. Even though I had to do the spiritual work for myself, I also really did need the help.

When I was in high school, I got to take a rock-climbing class. One of the most important things I learned in that class was the role of the belayer. Whenever one of us was climbing, someone else had to belay, holding the safety rope that was attached to the climber's harness. But the belayer wasn't just there for safety. When one of us got stuck, we could ask our belayer if they saw anything that was helpful for us. They'd say things like, "There's a good hold up to your left; if you shift to your right leg, you'll be able to reach it . . ." The belayer could often see things about our own route that we couldn't, because of the angle of our head or how close we were to the wall. Even though we had to make the moves for ourselves, the belayer could help. Likewise, in our life with God, we're in the thick of our own experience, close to the wall. Someone else—whether it's a spiritual director, a counselor, or a friend—can point us toward footholds we can't see for ourselves.

Deepening Friendship

Letting others help me find my footholds has changed the nature of my relationships. Dallas writes, "When I ask someone to do or to be or to give something, I stand with that person in the domain of a constraint without force or necessitation. We are together. A request by its very nature unites." To put the same thought in Brené Brown's terms, the authenticity of asking for help leads to genuine connection. Because I leave the other person truly free to respond to my request with a "yes" or "no," the request is a genuine admission of need, and the "yes" that often comes is a gift. Both sides of this dynamic lead to deeper trust. In my life, I've seen how asking for help leads to greater intimacy. I've gained relationships that simply didn't exist in my life before, as with George becoming my spiritual director. Other friendships have deepened.

One week, when Katie and I were in a particularly difficult place, my friend Neph and I decided to meet up at Chick-Fil-A. As we sat down at a bright red-and-white table with milkshakes and fries, I did most of the talking. I didn't have clarity about what was going on, or what I should do, so I just talked about everything in a meandering way that was probably as convoluted as I felt at the time. Neph listened, and asked a few questions, and mostly just reminded me that I was someone who mattered. He helped. And in helping, he became a closer and more important friend in my life.

Unfortunately, many people don't have a Neph in their life.

There are forces at work in Western society that mitigate the development of intimacy among friends. In a 2016 poll in the United Kingdom, almost one in five respondents said that they felt lonely often or all of the time. One in eight people said that they had no close friends at all. This trend is on the rise, as well; only half that many said they had no friends in a 2010 poll. On our side of the pond, scholar Robert Putnam has identified a trend of decreasing "social capital" in the United States over several decades. People do not interact with one another in community as they used to. The factors that contribute to these trends are complex, but I appreciate how Putnam identifies even the practical influence of the need for cars in the suburbs: "One inevitable consequence of how we have come to organize our lives spatially is that we spend measurably more of every day shuttling alone in metal boxes among the vertices of our private triangles." Whatever the causes, with decreased community life, we have fewer people to turn to for help when we need it.

As Katie and I have shuttled along the vertices of our private suburban triangles, we've had the unusual opportunity to make them a little less private. When we had been married for about three years, we and some friends of ours from church started talking about living together in community. It started as a joke: Dan and Joy O'Reagan were looking for a better situation than their current apartment, and someone said, "Why don't we move in together?" We laughed, and then we realized it wasn't half a bad idea. Katie and I were renting a small room from another growing family, so this wasn't our first foray into shared living arrangements. But with Dan and Joy, who were closer to our own age, we were able to take the time to plan our life together more thoughtfully and intentionally. We talked about what we each cared about in a home environment, and what it might look like to share groceries, host friends and family, and protect space for each family. There seemed to be real potential for us to craft an arrangement that would work for everyone.

After a few exploratory conversations, we had a check-in meeting where a couple of surprises came to light. On the Easley side of things, Katie had relapsed into her eating disorder, and she was headed into a full-time, outpatient program for eating recovery. We realized her complex needs would necessarily affect our community life if we did end up living together with the O'Reagans. So we shared with them the details of her needs, her treatment, and how unpredictable our road ahead looked. We still wanted to try this quirky domestic experiment, if they were up for it. Dan and Joy listened with empathy as they absorbed the details. Then they began asking questions like, "How could we best support you if we were still to do this? What would Katie need in the house?" Our needs did not scare them off. They wanted to figure out how to make it work.

They also had some O'Reagan news to share: they were expecting their first child! Now it was their turn to ask if we were still up for doing life together, given how much having a baby in the mix could change things. Katie and I were delighted, and then began asking Dan and Joy the same kinds of questions they had asked us. Now, for our part it was probably more a matter of perspective than generous character; the family we were renting from at the time had gone from four kids to a rambunctious six while we were staying with them. The prospect of living with just one tiny human seemed luxurious!

So, the five of us (counting the baby on the way) forged ahead with our planning. We began looking at houses where we could afford to split the rent. We settled on a three-bedroom ranch not far from our work and church. Katie and I moved in first, and then

Dan and Joy joined when their lease was up. As it happened, Katie was in the middle of a leave of absence from work (described in chapter three) right when they arrived. She was involved in medical and mental health treatment of one kind or another for eight hours a day. Joy was eight months pregnant; the baby came only five weeks after they moved in. None of us were in a place where we could hide much of our lives from each other. We had to ask one another for help all the time. But we did, and it worked. Inevitably, we became closer to one another in the process.

Having access to a garage for the first time since leaving home for college, Dan decided to take up woodworking. The first piece he made was a sign to hang in our front entryway, bearing the nickname we had given the arrangement: O'Easley. Their baby, a girl named Caitlyn, was baptized that Easter. Dan and Joy asked us to be her godparents. Caitlyn has brought joy and life to all of us in so many ways, from her hairy head to her curious face, which usually bears a confident smile. As Katie's health stabilized over the course of our first year together, Dan and Joy supported us all throughout the process. When she needed space, she could find it, and when we wanted to talk about things, Dan and Joy listened. In hindsight, it's hard to imagine how we would have made it through that year without Dan and Joy's steadiness in the background.

Suffice it to say, O'Easley is an unusual way of doing life in the suburbs. We're not a commune, and we do protect time and space for each family to have their own life. We share a grocery budget and one kitchen, but we're very thankful the house has two separate bathrooms! We each work normal jobs. But when we come home in the evening, we come home to each other more often than not. When we have friends over, we entertain together. We have house dinner one night a week, when we share what we're thankful for and talk through how "house things" are going and if anything needs to change. We often share other meals, too. At this point, we're more like extended family than friends in many ways.

For many people, living in community like we do may not be a practical option. It may take a certain kind of person; Katie and I were lucky to have friends like Dan and Joy who were willing to pursue something so unusual in such a thoughtful way. But everyone needs to learn how to ask for help boldly and creatively. As Western culture continues to suffer from decreased social trust, and people find themselves isolated in times of need, we as followers of Jesus can help lead the way in building connections that matter. It doesn't take a grand vision or expertise in community development. It just takes asking for help.

How to Ask

Asking for help can be a daunting proposition all by itself. For some people (like Brené Brown), grand vision and expertise may even seem easier. Even so, we have to put ourselves in that place of vulnerability if we're going to get the help we need. We have to learn how to ask.

A great place to start is with concrete opportunities that are right in front of you. If there is some routine opportunity in your life when you are invited to ask for help, consider participating the next time it comes up. At my church, every week the pastor invites people to go get prayer from one of our prayer team members at the side of the sanctuary. For me, this is a chance to ask for help which pops up every seven days. So often, though, I come up with a reason not to go get prayer: I'm busy with work responsibilities on Sundays, I should let other people who "need it more" get prayer, and so on.

Sometimes those excuses are valid, but sometimes they're not. I remember once being at church for a special conference. I was just attending a certain session; I had no work responsibilities. Our pastor invited anyone who wanted to come forward and receive prayer from a member of the prayer team, which was especially large for this event. He mentioned a specific matter for prayer: asking for a blessing for your spiritual gifts. I thought, "I could really use that." Even so, I didn't immediately get up out of my seat. I looked to see how it was going first. It was clear there were plenty of prayer team members; if I went forward, I wouldn't be depriving anyone else of their chance to get prayer. So, I finally got up out of my seat, walked a few feet forward . . . and then sat down again in another seat. I stayed there for about ten minutes before finding the courage to go and ask for prayer.

Something in me would always prefer to be the one praying for others rather than the one receiving prayer. If I go and get prayer, everyone will see that I'm the kind of person who needs prayer! What will they think of me? But of course, all of us are the kind of people who need prayer. So with routine invitations like the one I get every Sunday morning, all I need is courage.

Consider the routine opportunities for help that lie before you. If your church offers prayer ministry, go get prayed for. If you're a student at a campus with a free counseling center, go get counseling. Even if you're not sure you need to, just talk to the prayer minister or counselor about something that bothers you. You might be surprised at what happens in the process.

It's possible you don't have a ready-made chance to ask for help like that. If that's your situation, you'll need not only courage, but creativity, too. The creativity will come in determining who to ask for help, and how, and when. One option is to follow the pattern of this book so far: consider a feeling you have that seems particularly important, say, sadness about a difficult situation, or joy in a project you're working on. Then give attention to how that emotion might be related to a deeper need in your soul. Finally, try to think of a safe person who might understand what you're talking about if you were to ask them for help in meeting that need. Maybe grab coffee with them and talk about what's been making you sad. Or, invite someone else to help you in some practical way with your project, and talk to them about why you enjoy it so much while you work together.

Someone Who Knew How to Ask

In his book *Tuesdays with Morrie*, journalist Mitch Albom tells the story of re-connecting with Morrie Schwartz, a college professor who had been influential in Mitch's younger life. Morrie was dying, and Mitch decided to go spend time with him every Tuesday, ask him questions, and talk about what makes life meaningful. There's a kind of wisdom in Mitch's initiative; he knew that spending time with this old, thoughtful man would be a blessing. Mitch was willing to ask for help. But Morrie, it turns out, showed an even deeper kind of asking-for-help wisdom:

As his body weakened, the back and forth to the bathroom became too exhausting, so Morrie began to urinate into a large beaker. He had to support himself as he did this, meaning someone had to hold the beaker while Morrie filled it.

Most of us would be embarrassed by all this, especially at Morrie's age. But Morrie was not like most of us. When some of his close colleagues would visit, he would say to them, "Listen, I have to pee. Would you mind helping? Are you okay with that?"

Often, to their own surprise, they were.

That is a picture of the kind of asking for help we can aspire to. Free from pride, humble, and direct. It's the kind of asking for help that calls forth the best from other people and allows for gracious human connection. It's the kind of asking for help that God wants for us, so that he can show us just how generous he is.

The Lord as Helper

When we ask other people for help and find blessing in their response, it's the character of God himself that we're discovering. Throughout time, God's people have seen his generosity as they've received help for the most practical of needs. When something "went their way," they would offer up gratitude to God for his favor, rather than simply chalking it up to other people's goodwill or sheer luck. In the story of Israel, we see this pattern whenever the oppressors and enemies of God's people were overthrown. Even after the people themselves had marched into battle and won the day, they saw the victory as a gift from God:

> *Thus the* LORD *gave to Israel all the land that he swore to give to their fathers. And they took possession of it, and they settled there. And the* LORD *gave them rest on every side just as he had sworn to their fathers. Not one of all their enemies had withstood them, for the* LORD *had given all their enemies into their hands. Not one word of all the good promises that the* LORD *had made to the house of Israel had failed; all came to pass.* JOSHUA 21:43-45 ESV

Now, I imagine even in that ancient, spiritually-conscious culture, there were probably soldiers and families who had more of a skeptical attitude. It would be easy to attribute the victory to human intelligence, the mistakes of the enemy, or any number of factors. But the writer of this passage is saying, "Don't miss out on the meaning of this good turn. God is for you!"

In other words, God is helping us. He is a good, generous Father who delights to give us good gifts. We can count on his help. As we ask for help from others, we take a step toward receiving God's loving favor through them. And as our confidence in his generosity increases, we are moved to keep asking for help. This confidence changes our prayers as well, giving us faith to ask for whatever we need.

We, too, can receive the good things of life as signs of God's kindness toward us. We, too, can learn to say, "The Lord is my helper" (Hebrews 13:6 NIV, cf. Psalm 118:7).

When Help Hurts

Sometimes asking for help does not turn out the way we had hoped. It's possible for someone to say no, and depending on the relationship and the request, that rejection can lead to real hurt. It's also possible for someone to say yes, but in a way that ultimately dishonors us and our needs. When someone responds to our vulnerability by breaking trust, we rightly feel betrayed. That betrayal is all the more crushing when it comes from someone we should have been able to trust: a parent, a close friend, a pastor.

If you've been hurt by someone who should have helped you, you are not alone. Others have been hurt, too. Others can hear your story.

Even if we haven't been deeply hurt, the most trustworthy of people will at times disappoint us when we ask for help. So, what do we do then? It can be tempting to close ourselves off, to become self-sufficient. If we limit ourselves to what we can personally control, maybe we'll never have to ask for help again. Maybe we won't have to be vulnerable.

If you're in that place of just trying to protect yourself, then there is good news. You don't have to be vulnerable quickly. You don't have to open up broadly. You don't have to go faster or further than you're ready to go. You just have to take the next step.

Dan Allender, whose words on joy we read in chapter two, is a survivor of childhood sexual abuse. He shares his counsel on taking that next step toward help for fellow survivors, and I find his words to be more broadly relevant to all of us, as we seek the help of trustworthy people in our lives: "I recommend that you search high and low, pray and ponder, until you find a person who is neither judgmental and expecting rapid change, nor condescendingly sympathetic and concerned only with your victimization. Trust is neither something to expect nor to give too quickly; therefore, listen to your intuition, your hunch as to a person's capacity and willingness to hear."

We all need someone like that. When we take the risk of sharing our hidden hurts with a trustworthy confidant, we open the gate to healing. When we do so with an openness to God's presence and his people, we find he can minister salvation from even the deepest of wounds. Much more deserves to be said on this topic, but for now, know that help doesn't have to hurt. It can be true, and real, and full.

We all long for the kind of person whom we can ask to journey with us in that way. Someone who accepts us, and wants the best for us. Someone who will let us climb the rocks, but who holds tight to the belay. These are the kind of people who make asking for help really worth it. As we step out with courage, with creativity, and with confidence in God's provision, I'm persuaded we'll find people like this. I've found them in my life, and you can find them in yours. So find them. And then—ask for help.

CHAPTER 6

WAITING

When I proposed to Katie, I knew we probably couldn't get married within the next few months. I had wondered whether I should wait till we were a bit older, or at least until a wedding would be less than a year away. But I had already settled in my soul that I wanted to marry her, so I decided to go ahead and ask. She said yes, an answer for which I am continually grateful. (Our friends still can't figure out what she was thinking.) Once we got around to looking at wedding dates, we realized the earliest that would work was fifteen months after the proposal.

Now, many people have waited much longer than fifteen months for something good and important. I have a friend who is applying to medical school. By the time she finishes her residency, a decade may have passed. She is playing the long-game. But to me, that fifteen-month engagement felt longer than a decade. I so wanted to be married to Katie. Waiting was more than hard.

Waiting is a kind of emotional time travel. It takes our present energy and applies it to something that will occur in the future. We can wait with dread, poisoning the present moment with a future evil. Or we can wait with eager expectation, crowning the present moment with a future good. But I've found that the joyful kind of waiting only comes easily when we know just how soon we'll get what we want. (And, as in the case of my engagement, sometimes not even then!) Anticipating Christmas or a birthday allows us to count down the days, confident of when the celebration will arrive. But when we're waiting for a good thing, and we don't know when it will come, we feel anxiety and pain instead of joy. "How long?" becomes the question we carry in our hearts.

That kind of waiting reveals our limitations. We can't press fast-forward on the universe, or somehow tug tomorrow closer by force of will. We have to depend upon the efforts of other people, who are imperfect and often slow. But this kind of waiting can also open up new possibilities in our life with God.

Waiting for the Healing of the Church

In the past several years, experiences at my home church have helped me begin to see that side of waiting. The church where I grew up is a place of rare and wonderful worship and life. Each year, I hear stories of those who have returned to God and to life in his church here in ways they simply could not have imagined before. People who have been ready to give up on the church or on faith itself have found something different here.

The "something different" can be hard to describe. One phrase we use to try and capture it is that we are a "three-streams" church:

we worship in the ancient sacramental stream of faith as Anglicans, in the evangelical stream as people of the Bible and the Gospel, and in the charismatic stream as people open to the Holy Spirit. That means that on a given Sunday, you'll find the clergy dressed in white robes, leading people in liturgical prayers and gathering at the altar to celebrate the mystery of the Eucharist. You'll also find people raising their hands in worship, going to receive the laying on of hands from a prayer minister at the sides of the room, or listening to a leader share a word of prophecy or a prayer for supernatural healing. In the sermon, you'll hear teaching from the Bible that calls people to faith in Jesus Christ—and on occasion there will even be an invitation to pray a version of the Sinner's Prayer and receive him as Savior and Lord.

We're a both-and community. We don't want to pick between what God is doing in the Bible and what he's doing at the altar, between how he ministers to the mind and how he heals the heart. We want to be open to the fullness of what he's doing, as much as we can be. Having grown up in this context, it's only gradually that I've come to realize how rare bringing these things together can be. It makes my heart ache that many Christians grow up without knowing the riches of one or more of these streams of God's work. To see them flowing together in the life of our community is powerful. It's not unusual for a visitor to cry their way through a service, overwhelmed by the beauty of what they are experiencing.

Over time, I've also realized something else about our community: we are overwhelmingly white and middle-class. To a certain extent, this is due to our geographic location in the largely-white, western suburbs of Chicago. But as those suburbs have continued to deepen in ethnic diversity, our congregation has stayed behind the curve. This tendency to not keep up with trends of ethnic change is not unusual among U.S. churches, which for many reasons often develop an inner culture that reflects the norms of a particular racial demographic. According to Duke University's National Congregations Study, "Eighty-six percent of American congregations (containing 80 percent of religious service attendees) remain overwhelmingly white or black or Hispanic or Asian[.]" The reasons for such divisions are more complex than I can discuss here, but they have roots in longstanding racial injustice in U.S. history, both inside and outside the walls of the church. The racial fissures of our broader culture run right through our sanctuaries, too.

When I was a child, our church had a Latino congregation, but it disintegrated following a leadership crisis. When our senior pastor announced this difficult news to us, he admitted he bore some responsibility for not having maintained a closer relationship with the Latino pastor. He also mentioned that his ignorance of Spanish contributed to this relational distance. I must have only been about ten years old at the time of this announcement, but it stuck with me. In eighth grade when I had to choose what language to study, I chose Spanish. I didn't want to remain at a distance from my Latino neighbors if I could help it.

When I was in high school, my attention turned more explicitly to the history of race in the United States. As part of a school trip, I had the opportunity to spend a couple of weeks with John Perkins, a leader in the Civil Rights movement and a pioneer of Christian community development. Reading his book With Justice for All gave me a vision of the church loving people in a diverse community. It made me want to live in that kind of church, to realize that vision.

A passage from Ezekiel I had read several years earlier took on fresh meaning for me. At the time that Ezekiel prophesied, the people of God had been divided into two kingdoms, Israel and Judah, for hundreds of years. But God tells Ezekiel to take two sticks, and write "Judah" on one and "Israel" on the other, and bind them together in his hand. Then he says this:

> *"Thus says the Lord GOD: I will take the people of Israel from the nations among which they have gone, and will gather them from every quarter, and bring them to their own land. I will make them one nation in the land, on the mountains of Israel; and one king shall be king over them all. Never again shall they be two nations, and never again shall they be divided into two kingdoms."* EZEKIEL 37:21-22 NRSV

To me, this prophecy spoke of hope for God's reconciling work over all the divisions of his people, including the divisions that have resulted from racial injustice here in the United States. Passages like this stoked my yearning to be a part of that reconciliation even as it was taking place.

Stuck

As all this was happening, I was also settling into the conviction that I was called to be a pastor. Early on, mentors and pastors had called forward my gifts as a teacher and a leader and had encouraged my passion for seeing others come to a deeper knowledge of God. As I matured, it became clear to me and to almost everyone who personally knew me that pastoral ministry was part of what I was meant to do. I also had started to pay more attention to the sacramental/evangelical/charismatic tradition in which I was raised, and became convinced that both-and was the right approach whenever possible in doing church life. I wanted to keep living the both-and life I had been shown in my home church, but I wanted the people involved to be both-and, too: men and women, rich and poor, black and white and Latino and whoever else the Lord might bring along.

So, even before graduating from high school, I had the sense that I somehow wanted to serve as a pastor in a three-streams church involving people of many backgrounds and races. I also felt a tug toward trying to plant a church like this. Fast-forward to my college graduation, and my sense of vocation remained largely unchanged. A full-time staff position at my church opened up, and I decided to take it. From that home base, I then started trying to figure out how to move toward a more multicultural pattern of life. I began leading our church's refugee ministry, building a friendship with a local family from Burma. I started attending Wednesday night Bible study at a historical African-American congregation just a few miles down the road from our church. I also got involved with a Thursday-night ministry focusing on former prisoners and prisoners' families, which turned out to be one of the most racially and socioeconomically diverse communities I had encountered in the suburbs. I was starting to build some meaningful relationships with people rather unlike myself. It was encouraging. Then Katie and I had our speed bump conversation.

In order to love my wife, I had to cut down on my responsibilities outside of work. I've already written of how the decision to simplify my life paid off in unexpected ways for the good my soul and my marriage. But another side effect of this simplification has been the re-homogenization of my social network; I had to spend less time in communities besides my home church, which meant spending more time with white, middle class people. Despite my relative lack of experience in cross-cultural patterns of life, I knew that relationships form the core of any meaningful endeavor. This turn away from time in other communities and toward more time at my home church felt like a step backward rather than forward. I was continuing to invest in relationships with people like me rather than building new friendships with those who are different. To an extent, I enjoyed the benefits of being anchored in a community that knew me. But in another way I felt like I was stuck in the mud, prevented from taking steps toward a future multicultural vocation.

In the summer months following my conversation with Katie, I frequently prayed about this situation. Was I somehow misreading my responsibilities? Was I really supposed to stay involved in communities beyond my home church? I didn't want to keep trying to cram in those connections into my schedule to the detriment of my marriage. On the other hand, if my sense that I needed to step back was right, why was God depriving me of opportunities to build diverse friendships? Why would he give me such a strong sense of where my life was supposed to go, only to keep me from going anywhere?

As I wrestled with these questions, I tried to problem-solve the situation in an orderly manner. The problem: having a full-time job in a largely white church and actually spending time with my wife allowed me little margin for building relationships elsewhere. The attempt to have my cake and eat it too wasn't working. So, I reasoned, perhaps the solution would be to leave my home church entirely, seeking a new job and a more diverse faith community. I began exploring options, writing to a pastor I respected of a multicultural church in Seattle. I also talked with a friend of mine nearer to home, who invited me to join the staff of his young church plant and focus on college ministry in Chicago.

Meanwhile, Katie was gearing up for a one-year bachelor's completion program to begin that fall, having finished an associates nursing program earlier in the year. After her surgery in the summer, she relapsed into her eating disorder. As I wrote about in chapter three, I grappled with fear in new ways as Katie dropped out of school, took a leave of absence from work, and attended an eating recovery program. The reality check of Katie's needs made both of us take a break from any plans for re-locating or changing our jobs or church home.

Still, the vocational questions that had been nagging me didn't evaporate. It felt like God had grounded me, like a parent would a mischievous teenager: "Stay home." Why would he be doing this? How could this season of staying in one (rather white) place have anything to do with a vocation for multicultural life and ministry? I chafed against the sense of limitation. Feeling confused, I sought the counsel of several people whom I knew could speak to me frankly and fairly. Joel, a friend from Miami with lots of multicultural ministry experience, spent an afternoon listening to my story. He affirmed my struggle and validated how stuck I felt. Then he said, "Well, Chris, I've known a lot of white people who have gotten involved in multicultural work. Most of them eventually flame out because the experience doesn't measure up to their ideal of how it ought to work. The ones who are able to stick with it, through all of its slow and imperfect realities, are those who have been through the fire at some point in their lives. Suffering shapes people. What you and Katie are going through is preparing you for the future."

In other words, Joel said that waiting might be a good thing. That God could fashion me into a man more ready for multi-cultural ministry, even in a mono-cultural season. That his purposes were not going away just because they weren't getting fulfilled immediately. That suffering with and caring for Katie wasn't meaningless.

That is not what I wanted to hear. But I trusted Joel, so I did my best to adopt a new attitude. Waiting was okay, I told myself. I don't have to solve this problem. I can stay where I am, and take care of Katie. I applied all my powers of soul to staying rooted.

I lasted about three months. Then I had the brilliant idea that

Katie and I could relocate, not to Chicago or Seattle, but just down the road to Aurora! My pastor friend Trevor had recently led a team to plant a church there, and the community was much more diverse. I could switch church jobs while Katie was still in school, get more cross-cultural experience, and everything would be peachy. I scheduled a meeting with Trevor to convince him to let me join up.

Thank God, Trevor immediately wised up to what was going on for me. Instead of brainstorming with me about how I could get involved in Aurora, he asked, "Why not wait?"

I was taken aback. Wait? But I'd been waiting for so long already! "Why don't you take the year off from seminary?" he asked. "Why don't you take a year off from planning the next thing?" Both of those ideas sounded crazy to me. Not only was he suggesting I not immediately move toward multicultural pastoral ministry; he was suggesting that I go a whole year without even planning the next step.

As Trevor continued to talk and listen, somehow what he and Joel and Katie and others had been trying to get through to me finally settled in. A year to just be where I already was sounded inviting, in a strange way. What if God didn't want me to move forward frenetically? What if he wanted me to wait?

When I came home, I shared Trevor's thoughts with Katie. "I think he might have a point," I admitted.

"No kidding!" Katie said.

So it was that Katie and I decided to take what we called a Sabbath year. I took twelve months off from school, and Katie took twelve months off from work. In the summer, she re-enrolled in her school program and just focused on that, while I continued my job at the church. We cut out all of my routine leadership responsibilities outside of my job. I canceled my Friday appointments and began taking that day as a more robust Sabbath in the week than

I had ever practiced before: no work, no ministry, no chores. Just time with Katie, time in nature, time with friends, and a little bit of prayer. I also labored manfully not to make plans for the next year, and I made it nine months on that, too. (Katie, and the Lord, were merciful about me not making it quite till the end.)

Sabbath year became the single most powerful spiritual decision of our lives up to that point. It opened up time to tend to our souls and our marriage. It made me aware of how joyful life could be even when I'm not constantly getting things done. It wrested from me the power of following the plan, and I discovered that God still took care of us.

It also deepened my faith, as God suddenly started doing the things I was longing for without me even lifting a finger. In August of our Sabbath year, the atrocity of racist violence in Charlottesville, Virginia broke open deeper discussion around race at our church. In response, our pastor invited Michael, an African-American partner in ministry, to come preach that October. We'd had many African preachers visit our church before, but that was the first time a black American preached in our sanctuary. Pastor Michael preached on race relations in the church and gave a powerful call to revival through renewed relationship. He then led a process by which members of our church could begin visiting and building relationships with the people of black congregations on the West Side of Chicago. Dozens of people participated.

In hindsight, if I had "succeeded" in moving to Seattle in order to get more multicultural experience, I would have missed out on how God began to work powerfully along those lines in my home community. If Trevor had let me work with him in Aurora, I wouldn't have discovered the beauty of Sabbath year. If I had rushed ahead into what I believed I was called by God to do, I would have lost what he was actually doing in my heart. God's power was available for his purposes, but he could not deliver it through my impatient plans. I had to discard my plans, and obey him by waiting in order to receive what he was giving me, and participate in what he was giving to my broader church community. Only by being a "bad" multicultural Christian, "stuck" in a white church, could I move toward becoming the kind of Christian that I so longed to be, letting God's life flow through me.

How Waiting Works

Catholic priest and contemplative writer Henri Nouwen considers waiting within the Gospel accounts that lead up to Jesus' birth:

A waiting person is a patient person. The word "patience" means the willingness to stay where we are and live the situation out to the full in the belief that something hidden there will manifest itself to us. . . . Patient living means to live actively in the present and wait there. Waiting, then, is not passive. It involves nurturing the moment, as a mother nurtures the child that is growing in her womb. Zechariah, Elizabeth, Mary, Simeon, and Anna were present to the moment. That is why they could hear the angel. They were alert, attentive to the voice that spoke to them and said, "Don't be afraid. Something is happening to you. Pay attention."

Waiting allows us to see what God is doing here and now, not just then and there. It brings our focus to the realities of the people around us and of the places where we live and work. It encourages our curiosity. Instead of asking, "When can I get out of here?" we ask, "What might God be doing?" And then we listen for his response and how he is inviting us into his rest and his work. Waiting delivers us from an unhealthy idealism into the true ideals of obedience.

Early twentieth-century preacher Oswald Chambers said,

"Beware of outstripping God by your very longing to do his will. We run ahead of Him in a thousand and one activities, consequently we get so burdened with persons and with difficulties that we do not worship God, we do not intercede." Disliking waiting as much as I do, I often find myself "outstripping God" in this way. I want to move quickly, sometimes more quickly than he does. Waiting allows me to keep in step with the Spirit. Nothing is more urgent than staying connected to God, than growing up into the maturity of deeper worship and surrender to God. The way of waiting gives us the slow, peaceful pattern of focus upon God, not just what we want to do for him.

All throughout the Scriptures, we see stories of quiet waiting in which God makes himself known. One that's always inspired me is the story of Joseph from the book of Genesis. Joseph, like me, had "golden boy" status in his community as a young man. He was favored to grow in influence and authority. He had a vision of his future, full of glory and renown. He was, perhaps, a little full of himself. His brothers sold him into slavery out of jealousy, and with little warning, Joseph entered into a hard, years-long trial of servitude and later imprisonment.

Those years as a slave and a prisoner are hard for me to imagine, having lived with such abundance and privilege all of my life. What must it have been like to feel the humiliation of being treated as property by his captors, the physical pain of the abuse he must have suffered, the pangs of hunger in a dark prison cell? How often did he wonder, "How long?" It must have been tempting to fall into bitterness, anger, or despair. Yet the Bible tells us that Joseph, somehow, responded to the difficulties of his circumstances with fortitude. He became a leader even within the prison in which he was confined:

But the LORD was with Joseph and showed him steadfast love and gave him favor in the sight of the keeper of the prison. And the keeper of the prison put Joseph in charge of all the prisoners who were in the prison. Whatever was done there, he was the one who did it. The keeper of the prison paid no attention to anything that was in Joseph's charge, because the LORD was with him. And whatever he did, the LORD made it succeed. GENESIS 39:21-23 ESV

Through an unexpected and miraculous series of events, Joseph was eventually launched from the lowly status of prisoner to a senior administrative post in the most powerful empire in the world at that time. From that post, he made arrangements that saved thousands of lives— including those of his brothers and relatives, adding an unexpected chapter of forgiveness and reconciliation to his family's story. His vision of exercising authority and influence was fulfilled, but more beautifully and abundantly than he could have imagined.

I have often pondered the purposes of God in leaving Joseph to wait in that prison cell for so long before that happy ending. For years, Joseph's day-by-day obedience was not the dramatic actions that would save an empire, but the minutiae of organizing life with his fellow prisoners. Joseph learned to look for what God was doing even there, in a thankless job, far from home. I wonder if it was that spiritual lesson that prepared him for the responsibilities he would inherit in the empire.

Joseph's life of waiting follows the pattern of a story Jesus told, in which a king says to his slave, "Well done, good servant! Because you have been faithful in a very little, you shall have authority over ten cities" (Luke 19:17 ESV). Joseph was faithful with little, so God put him over much. But I think it's easy to miss the point in this kind of story. It's not like Joseph earned the greater responsibility by being faithful with the smaller things, as though God was seeing if he measured up. The ten cities of Jesus' story are not that kind of reward. No, I think that Joseph became the kind of person who can lead with humility and grace while he was in that prison. God set Joseph over an empire because he had matured to a point where he could be trusted with one.

That kind of spiritual transformation, from the golden boy with a swagger to the calm and generous ruler, can only happen through waiting. That is what God has in store for each of us, if we are willing to participate. He wants to make us the kind of people to whom he can entrust great things. But the only way he can do it is by making us wait for those great things, giving us the small things we are truly ready for. That means that, no matter how big the dream God has given us, the way forward will often consist in everyday and unimpressive acts of obedience.

For me, those simple acts of obedience often come at home. Caring for my wife forces me to stay in one place. It puts me face to face with my own weaknesses and limitations, as I have so little control over whether she is well or ill. It allows me to love in a way that scores no points. While personal ambition gets so easily mixed in to more impressive forms of ministry, taking care of Katie does nothing to establish my public reputation. The day-in, day-out details of loving Katie don't gratify my desire for concrete ministry success. Instead, the work of marriage itself is shaping my heart and my habits. As I give more of my time to tasks which confer on me no glory—doing the dishes, cleaning the bathroom, sharing time in the car—I'm also giving them more weight in my vision of what really matters in the universe. It's not just my projects at work or even my sense of ministry vocation that matters. There is a person, right in front of me, who matters, not because of what she can do for me or how she fits into some grand scheme, but simply for her own sake. In the end, that is how every person matters. That is what ministry is really about, and what all the projects and productivity must serve. The great things that God calls us into are ways to love and care for other people more and more fully.

Ultimately, waiting can become for us what the Bible calls waiting for the Lord. In Isaiah, we read the prayer

> *O LORD, be gracious to us; we wait for you.*
> *Be our arm every morning,*
> *our salvation in the time of trouble.*
>
> ISAIAH 33:2 NRSV

When we're waiting, something has not yet arrived. Like Joseph in that prison cell, we're waiting for salvation, for deliverance from the trouble. But we're not just waiting for any change of circumstance; we're waiting for God's deliverance. We want him to be our arm every morning, to be himself within us the strength we need for the day ahead. When we offer our waiting itself to the Lord, we remember that we need him even more than whatever else we are waiting for. In that moment, waiting becomes worship.

Looking Ahead

I still feel a long ways away from the vision of pastoring a three-streams church that brings together the races and cultures of our communities. God is doing something mysterious and exciting in drawing my home church into cross-cultural relationship. At the same time, overall, we're still pretty white and middle class. Our cultural mores remain largely unchanged, and we know better than to think the long and fraught history of U.S. church and race relations will be transformed overnight. We are at the beginning of an adventure led by the Spirit, not the end. My own personal social network reflects that reality, too. While I keep learning new things from other congregations and building new friendships, for now, the majority of my friends and partners in ministry share my own racial and cultural background. I'm still waiting for the healing of the church, and my chance to participate in it.

But I no longer feel the same urgency I once did to "make things happen," to force my way into a more multicultural context, to fulfill the vision through my own capacities for getting things done and following the plan. I have to trust that doing what I need to for the sake of my own soul, and to care for Katie, will find its way back into the purposes of God for his vision of multicultural life and ministry. I'm still bad at waiting. I don't like it. But by God's grace, I'm learning to wait for him. And when I do, he shows up.

Conclusion

I'M NOT OUT OF THE WOODS YET. Even while writing this book, I've felt the force of my two laws like a weight on my shoulders. The shame that drives me to get things done and the fear that makes me follow the plan haven't disappeared from my mind and heart, even if they're less powerful than they used to be. The habit of trying to measure up still feels automatic. When I write, I still hear the voice that says, "You'd better get it right, or else." As I pen this conclusion, I'm six months beyond the date I originally set for publication. When I fall behind on my own goals like that, the anxiety kicks in. What if I never get it done? What if it's not worth sharing? How will it all come together?

I feel the tug of the plan, telling me I can force reality into my schemes, even though I know such control is an illusion. I'm tempted to define myself by what I get done, even though I know God's gracious love, not my productivity, is the source of who I am. Even after setting these laws aside, I find myself looking at them, picking them up, trying them on for size. Before I know it, I'm back into the project of being a good Christian. I push for external results, either to impress others or to satisfy my own demands, neglecting the internal life of joy and rest that Jesus invites me to practice with him.

But I'm hopeful. Signs of God's faithfulness abound. As I write these words, Katie is softly playing guitar in our living room. She's in better health than we could have hoped for, given some of the scares we've had along the way. Day to day, she has bright eyes, with energy enough to serve as a nurse and still make time for her friends and family in the way she's always wanted to. She was awarded employee of the quarter last week at the hospice center where she works. She eats well.

Eight months out from the end of Sabbath year, our marriage is also in good health. Even though the pace of ministry has picked up for me, I'm not distracted from Katie's needs like I once was. (And when I am, she's quick to point it out.) I'm more consistently giving her attention, and receiving it from her, whether in conversation at the end of the day or when we're out for a date. Some of the habits of Sabbath year, like a well-protected weekly Sabbath day, we're carrying with us for the long run. Marriage is messy, and negative emotions still surface for me just as much as ever, but I'm learning to be present to them. When times are tough, I'm now quick to reach out for help, whether by talking to my counselor or a friend. And when painful questions remain unanswered, I'm learning to live in the tension, loving Katie faithfully while we wait for what's next.

These signs of life make me curious. What if I'm still just getting started? When I fall back into the rhythm of my ministry disorder, what if I don't have to stay there? How might God be opening up new places in my heart even through hard experiences? How much further can I go in the practices of feeling, giving and receiving attention, asking for help, and waiting? What else is there to be discovered?

I don't think I'll regret asking questions like that. I don't think my hope for a fuller, better life will be disappointed. Because, as hard as it is to become a bad Christian, I have the best help in the world. The heart of the Christian life, as it's meant to be, is letting God's life flow through us. And that life is a gift, not something I have to earn or measure up to or plan or get done. It's a gift from the one who laid down his life for us. The very life of God coursed through Jesus' veins all the days of his life, and it's that life he poured out in his blood on the cross. It's that life he took up again on the third day, and gives freely to all who believe. It's the life he is giving to me, one day at a time, as I trust in him.

Jesus unmuddies the rivers of my soul just a little bit more, and just a little bit more, each time I open up to him. He teaches me to pray, "God, have mercy on me, a sinner" without shame. He wraps his arms around me and tells me, "Don't be afraid." I'm still learning to be a bad Christian. But I'm learning. The water is getting purer, and cleaner, and brighter. Yours can, too. Because Jesus is the one who feels with you, who gives you the attention you need, who helps you, and who waits with you.

Let his life flow through you.

Acknowledgements

A FEW WORDS at the back of the book are poor payment for so large a debt of gratitude that I owe to so many friends, colleagues, and partners in crime. Books are like gardens, and what fruit can be harvested from the preceding pages comes from many people's efforts to plant, weed, fertilize, and fence. Any remaining weeds and failed seedlings remain, of course, my responsibility.

Encouragement and criticism which decisively improved the text came from my exemplary team of readers: Alison Freeman, Bret Heddleston, Matt Woodley, Meghan Robins, Whitney Wiley, Drew Boa, and Josh Fort. Justin Cloyd went above and beyond, providing feedback on every chapter. (Justin's enthusiasm for the project also remained unmatched, and readers will have to judge whether I should have followed his advice to multiply most chapters and so double the length of the text.) Geoffrey Hagberg's meticulous editorial attention and keen eye for the work as a whole allowed me to revise nearly every paragraph.

Few self-published authors enjoy the influence of a true expert like Cindy Kiple, whose cover design makes the book look more professional than, perhaps, it truly is. Audra Nelessen's interior design also surpassed expectations to bring beauty and clarity to every page.

For a work that has grown up out of the painful and beautiful experiences Katie and I have had together over the last several years, thanks are due not only to collaborators in the project, but even more so to those who have shaped and sustained us through prayer, acts of service, patient listening, and "words in season" (Proverbs 15:23). We have been shepherded so faithfully by Val McIntyre, Kevin and Karen Miller, Matt Woodley, Brett Crull, and Trevor McMaken. George Ridgeway has carried on the labor of spiritual direction with patience and aplomb, while Chad Klopfenstein, Justin Cloyd, and Josiah Ostoich perfected the art in our group sessions. (Maybe next we can work on "How to Be a Bad Ignatian"?) Nephtali Matta has been there at the bleakest moments, and just by being there has made them far less bleak. Alison Freeman has served as cousin-in-residence par excellence while Dan, Joy, Caitlyn, and Peter O'Reagan have furnished a residence of *koinonia* we can't help but thank God for again and again. Mom and Dad Easley and Mom and Dad Walter, as usual, have sustained us with food and hospitality in and out of season. And Benjamin and David continue to put up with each of us, which is more than we can ask for.

Finally, Kippa. Words fail me. Thank you.

Notes

CHAPTER 1

1. *Gallup reports that the average work week:* Lyida Saad, "The '40-Hour' Workweek Is Actually Longer -- by Seven Hours," *Gallup News*, August 29, 2014, https://news.gallup.com/poll/175286/hour-workweek-actually-longer-seven-hours.aspx.
2. *Research from the Harvard Business Review:* Lieke ten Brummelhuis and Nancy P. Rothbard, "How Being a Workaholic Differs from Working Long Hours — and Why That Matters for Your Health," *Harvard Business Review*, June 14, 2018, https://hbr.org/2018/03/how-being-a-workaholic-differs-from-working-long-hours-and-why-that-matters-for-your-health.
3. *"She left her signature on us":* John Steinbeck, ". . . like captured fireflies," in *America and Americans and Selected Nonfiction*, ed. Susan Shillinglaw and Jackson J. Benson (New York: Penguin, 2002), 142-43.
4. *"the opposite of love is not hatred":* Read Mercer Schuchardt, "The Future of the Church Is Analog, Not Digital," *Christianity Today*, September 23, 2016, http://www.christianitytoday.com/ct/2016/october/future-of-church-is-analog-not-digital.html?start=5.

CHAPTER 2

1. *"that driving, grasping, fearful self-will":* Pete Scazzero, *Emotionally Healthy Spirituality: Unleash a Revolution in Your Life in Christ* (Nashville, TN: Thomas Nelson, 2006), 130-131.

CHAPTER 3

1. *The song "Please Be My Strength" by Michael Gungor:* Michael Gungor, "Please Be My Strength," track 9 on *Beautiful Things*, Brash Records, 2009, https://music.apple.com/us/album/please-be-my-strength/353582848?i=353582871.
2. *"Christians anger only rarely and only righteously":* Hugh Hewitt, *In, But Not Of:*

    A Guide to Christian Ambition and the Desire to Influence the World (Nashville: Thomas Nelson, 2003), 192.
3. *"Jesus is giving us a revelation of the preciousness of human beings":* Dallas Willard, *The Divine Conspiracy: Rediscovering Our Hidden Life in God* (San Francisco: HarperCollins, 1998), 154-55.
4. *"joy is different than happiness":* See, for example, Kay Warren's *Choose Joy: Because Happiness Isn't Enough* (Grand Rapids, MI: Revell, 2013), 139: "Happiness requires no effort on our part, but joy results from our deliberate choices to think differently, act differently and feel differently."
5. *"a joy in the midst of suffering":* Dan B. Allender and Tremper Longman III, *The Cry of the Soul: How Our Emotions Reveal Our Deepest Questions about God* (Colorado Springs: NavPress, 1994), 256-57.
6. *a book written by an influential pastor:* John Piper, *Don't Waste Your Life* (Wheaton, IL: Crossway, 2003), 45-46.
7. *I stole it from C.S. Lewis:* C.S. Lewis, *The Screwtape Letters* (London: Macmillan, 1945), 47.
8. *"my bones continue to be shaky, shriveled, eaten up":* John Fawcett, "Fighting Depression," John Fawcett's Blog, January 19, 2008, http://johnfawcett.blogspot.com/2008/01/fighting-depression.html.
9. *"As for one of the more positive things":* John Fawcett, "Special Need of Prayer," *John Fawcett's Blog*, March 11, 2008, http://johnfawcett.blogspot.com/2008/03/special-need-of-prayer.html.
10. *"I think I already mentioned":* John Fawcett, "The Joy of Boredom," *John Fawcett's Blog*, December 29, 2007, http://johnfawcett.blogspot.com/2007/12/joy-of-boredom.html.
11. *"I have walked a journey of bare-bones humanity":* Margie Fawcett, "Guide Us to Thy Perfect Light," *The Fruitful Vine* (blog), January 6, 2008, https://margiefawcett.blogspot.com/2007/12/guide-us-to-thy-perfect-light.html.
12. *"If you never allow yourself to feel the pain of loss":* Andrew Bauman, "The Pilgrimage of Grief," *The Allender Center at the Seattle School* (blog), June 18, 2015, https://theallendercenter.org/2015/06/pilgrimage-of-grief/.

CHAPTER 4

1. *to pay attention to God paying attention to me:* I'm indebted to Robert R. Marsh's "Looking at God Looking at You" for this idea, which I came across in the course of learning about the Ignatian Exercises under the leadership of Deacon Valerie McIntyre at Church of the Resurrection in Wheaton, Illinois. Robert R. Marsh, SJ. "Looking at God Looking at You: Ignatius' Third Addition," *The Way* 43, no. 4 (October 2004): 19-28, https://www.theway.org.uk/back/434Marsh.pdf.
2. *"You see, God doesn't wish to overwhelm":* Dallas Willard, "Spiritual Disciplines in a Postmodern World," interview by Luci Shaw, *Radix Magazine*, Spring 2000, 4-7 & 26-31, accessed March 18, 2018, http://www.dwillard.org/articles/artview.asp?artID=56.

3. *"The Cross is the abyss of wonders"*: Thomas Traherne, "The First Century," in *Centuries of Meditations*, 3-79 (London: Ballantyne & Limited, 1908), 41, https://www.ccel.org/ccel/traherne/centuries.i_1.html. My attention was first brought to Traherne's poem by Leanne Payne's *Listening Prayer* (Grand Rapids, MI: Baker, 1994).
4. *"No time is more profitably spent"*: Dallas Willard, "Personal Soul Care," in *The Pastor's Guide to Effective Ministry* (Kansas City, MO: Beacon Hill Press, 2002), accessed March 18, 2018, http://dwillard.org/articles/individual/personal-soul-care.
5. *"How do they paint one today?"*: Winston Churchill, quoted in Joseph L. Sax, *Playing Darts with a Rembrandt: Public and Private Rights in Cultural Treasures* (Ann Arbor: University of Michigan Press, 1999), 38.
6. the book You Are Special: Max Lucado, *You Are Special*, illustrated by Sergio Martinez (Wheaton, IL: Crossway, 1997).

CHAPTER 5

1. *"a strong sense of love and belonging"*: Brené Brown, "The Power of Vulnerability," filmed June 2010 at TEDxHouston, Houston, TX, video, 6:59, https://www.ted.com/talks/brene_brown_on_vulnerability.
2. *"Here's what I found"*: Brown, "Power of Vulnerability," 8:41.
3. *"I personally thought it was betrayal"*: Brown, "Power of Vulnerability," 10:44.
4. *"the ask-seek-knock teaching"*: Willard, *Divine Conspiracy*, 232.
5. *"In the very act of asking"*: Willard, *Divine Conspiracy*, 233.
6. *"When I ask someone"*: Willard, *Divine Conspiracy*, 233. Emphasis original.
7. they felt lonely often or all of the time: David Marjoribanks and Anna Darnell Bradley, "The Way We Are Now: You're not alone – the quality of the UK's social relationships" (Doncaster and Edinburgh: Relate and Relationships Scotland, March 2017), 14, https://www.relate.org.uk/sites/default/files/the_way_we_are_now_-_youre_not_alone.pdf.
8. they had no close friends at all: Marjoribanks and Bradley, "The Way We Are Now," 8.
9. only half that many: Marjoribanks and Bradley, "The Way We Are Now," 8.
10. *a trend of decreasing "social capital"*: Robert Putnam, *Bowling Alone* (New York: Touchstone Books, 2001).
11. *"One inevitable consequence . . ."*: Putnam, *Bowling Alone*, 212.
12. Mitch Albom tells the story of re-connecting with Morrie Schwartz: Mitch Albom, *Tuesdays with Morrie: An Old Man, a Young Man, and Life's Greatest Lesson* (New York: Doubleday, 1997).
13. *"As his body weakened"*: Albom, *Tuesdays with Morrie*, 11.
14. *"I recommend that you search high and low"*: Dan Allender, *The Wounded Heart: Hope for Adult Victims of Childhood Sexual Abuse*, rev. ed. (Colorado Springs: NavPress, 2008), 195.

CHAPTER 6
1. *"Eighty-six percent of American congregations":* Mark Chaves and Shawna L. Anderson, "Changing American Congregations: Findings from the Third Wave of the National Congregations Study," (Durham, NC: Department of Sociology, Duke University), 8, http://www.soc.duke.edu/natcong/Docs/Changing_American_Congs.pdf.
2. *"A waiting person is a patient person":* Henri J. M. Nouwen, *The Path of Waiting* (Chestnut Ridge, NY: Crossroad, 1995), 15-17.
3. *"Beware of outstripping God":* Oswald Chambers, *My Utmost for His Highest* (New York: Dodd, Mead, and Company, 1935), 92.

Made in the USA
San Bernardino, CA
22 July 2019